Empath is Not a Four-Letter Word

A guide for six-sensory people living in a five-sensory world
A personal journey of an awakening empath,
with conversations from the other side

SANDY WESTERMAN

Copyright © 2022 Sandy Westerman.

All rights reserved. No part of this book may be used or reproduced by any means, graphic, electronic, or mechanical, including photocopying, recording, taping or by any information storage retrieval system without the written permission of the author except in the case of brief quotations embodied in critical articles and reviews.

Balboa Press books may be ordered through booksellers or by contacting:

Balboa Press
A Division of Hay House
1663 Liberty Drive
Bloomington, IN 47403
www.balboapress.com
844-682-1282

Because of the dynamic nature of the Internet, any web addresses or links contained in this book may have changed since publication and may no longer be valid. The views expressed in this work are solely those of the author and do not necessarily reflect the views of the publisher, and the publisher hereby disclaims any responsibility for them.

The author of this book does not dispense medical advice or prescribe the use of any technique as a form of treatment for physical, emotional, or medical problems without the advice of a physician, either directly or indirectly. The intent of the author is only to offer information of a general nature to help you in your quest for emotional and spiritual well-being. In the event you use any of the information in this book for yourself, which is your constitutional right, the author and the publisher assume no responsibility for your actions.

Any people depicted in stock imagery provided by Getty Images are models, and such images are being used for illustrative purposes only. Certain stock imagery © Getty Images.

Print information available on the last page.

ISBN: 979-8-7652-2721-3 (sc)
ISBN: 979-8-7652-2722-0 (e)

Balboa Press rev. date: 06/22/2022

Ring the bells that still can ring
Forget your perfect offering
There is a crack, a crack in everything
That's how the light gets in
—Leonard Cohen

Contents

Preface xiii
Acknowledgments xv
Introduction xvii

Part One: Life Lessons
True Stories from the Life of an Empath

1. Superpowers 1
2. Thrown Off the School Bus 8
3. Overwhelmed in a Hallway 11
4. Who Does This Belong To? 13
5. Love in an Elevator 16
6. Choking in a Fancy Restaurant 20
7. A Deathbed Promise 23
8. A Poem 29
9. Babbling Psychosis 31
10. A Deer Miss 33
11. Code Strong 35
12. Wedding Visit 38
13. Gifts Wrapped Up as Visions from the Future 41
14. Don't Open the Door! 44
15. Overpass Collapse 46
16. Becoming a Fairy Grandmother 48
17. Mama 50
18. Conversations from the Other Side 56
19. More Conversations from the Other Side 62

20. Dreams..65
21. Heart Songs 67
22. Who Am I and What Am I Doing Here? 70

Part Two: Handbook
Your Brain's Operation Manual

23. Concentrate on What You Want..75
24. Get Off the Crazy Train 76
25. Listen to Your Words 77
26. Take Care of Your Body..78
27. Step Away from the Fire 80
28. Be Your Own Guru..81
29. Stay in the Present Moment..82
30. Go with the Flow 83
31. Making Decisions 84
32. Weird Is Cool..86
33. Understanding Ourselves 87

Part Three: Coming Home to Yourself
Practical Techniques You Can Use

34. Ground Yourself..91
35. Deep Belly Breathing...95
36. Becoming Present...97
37. Drink Water..99
38. Meditation...100

Part Four: Balancing Your Energies
Calming Yourself in the Storm

39. Meridians 107
    Tired, Give yourself a rub

40. Aura 109
41. Chakras 111

42. Resolving Common Problems with Energy Techniques...........112
    Feeling disconnected from your body, hook yourself up
    Exhausted, get your energies crossing over
    Mind in a fog, get unscrambled
    In Emotional Distress, hold your head
    For Anger
    For Fear
    For Grief
    For Panic
    For Worry
    For Stress
    Over Reacting, or Just Feeling Terrible
    Freak out Frenzy
        -a simple procedure to get cool calm and collected
    Bonus Exercise

43. Tapping 128

Epilogue 131
Suggested Reading 133
About the Author 135

I dedicate this book to *you*, dear reader. May you search through this book and find the gifts I left especially for you.

Preface

Why am I writing this book?

I am writing this book because my heart wants to be heard. I am writing this for *me*, because my story needs to be recorded. I am hoping this book will serve as a reassuring guide and inspiration to other sensitive people.

Imagine that you are an alien baby dropped off as an infant into a "normal" human family. As you grow up, you begin to realize that you are perceiving things no one else perceives. All of the people around you are oblivious to what you are experiencing. Even though you may have superpowers and abilities, it is easy, as a child, to feel that something is very wrong with you. Without guidance and instruction, life can get very confusing and overwhelming.

I am hoping that this book will serve the sensitive ones so that they will know that *sensitive* is the new strong, that their greatest weaknesses are also their greatest strengths, and that their special gifts are needed in this world. This book was created as a guide for six-sensory beings living in a five-sensory world. It is for my grandchildren, my special mentees, my loved ones, and for all the young people coming behind me.

I offer this as a way to lead others, clearing a path through the tangled dark woods as I hold a torch and light the way for you. I am writing this to serve as a true history of my struggles as I discovered my superpowers. May it be a blessing and a guide to you on *your* way.

Acknowledgments

I would like to thank my dear husband, Jeff Wolfson, for his meticulous editing of this book. Thank you for not only being my life partner but supporting me in everything I have tried to do.

I would also like to thank my wonderful big sis, Roz Westerman, for her grammatical expertise, for her encouragement, and for teaching me how to read. She has always been the best sister and friend anyone could hope to have, and I have been blessed to have her in my life.

I would like to give full credit and thanks to Donna Eden and David Feinstein. Donna and all of my amazing teachers from Eden Energy Medicine have taught me life-changing strategies for communicating with and balancing my own energies. I have tried to share some of these techniques with you in this book. David's linear influence has helped bring Donna's amazing work to the world.

Lastly, I would like to thank all of my family, friends, and teachers. Each of you is special to me, and you have made a difference in my life. I love you all and have purposely not mentioned specific names out of respect for your privacy.

Introduction

You may be wondering:
What is an empath exactly?
Am I an empath?

An empath is a person who has the ability to perceive information, sensations, or emotions that do not come from the usual five senses. In other words, empaths have the ability to receive signals or information that they do not see, hear, taste, smell, or touch.

We have learned that we humans have five senses. They are our way of functioning in our world. However, if you are reading this book, you are most probably aware that as Shakespeare said, "There are more things in heaven and earth." There are so-called coincidences, and perhaps you have had an unexplainable experience in your own life. This book explores some of the sixth senses, or the other ways we may experience things.

Those of us who are empaths may feel as if these extra sensitivities are a burden or a curse, much like a four-letter word. My hope is that this book will open your eyes to the gift that you are.

Part One
LIFE LESSONS

True Stories from the Life of an Empath

1

Superpowers

I HAD HEARD OF PEOPLE WHO lifted refrigerators or cars in dire emergencies, but I never imagined that I could have such "superhero" strength or that something like that would ever happen to me. After all, I was only seventeen years old at the time and never had been into any real exercise or muscle-building. If I weighed 104 pounds, that was a lot, because we barely ate. We lived on sunshine and pure joy.

It was the 1960s, and we had somehow convinced our parents that it would be a good idea to allow two teenage girls to spend a summer on their own, living at the beach. My buddy was named Eleanor; I nicknamed her Ellie. She had at least just graduated from high school, but I was only a junior. Even so, I was the leader, because I was taking *her* to the shore!

I had spent the previous summer at the beach in Atlantic City, New Jersey. This year, we were trying a brand-new beach: Ocean City, Maryland. We did no research and had no idea where we would live or work. We both lived in small, rural towns in Virginia, so two naïve young girls going out on their own was quite an exciting adventure.

We got a ride with an older male friend from home, and the only thing I remember about the four-hour drive was that we never stopped. We learned how far our bladders could stretch on that trip and the bursting sensation was unforgettable.

Our parents had given us a little money to get started, and with luggage in hand, we found a room with a bathroom to rent. It was a rundown space over a bar, with literal holes in the wall. I remember that there was a funny smell in the drawers.

We set out to find help-wanted signs, and I found a place to work on the boardwalk called Twirl a Paint. It was an open-air spin-art place. People would spill paint on a blank card and then spin it to make a painting. It was my job to keep the paint filled up in the little cups, take out the pictures, frame them, and keep the customers happy.

I did that last part really well, not only because I loved interacting with people, especially kids, but because I had special talents. You see, I could almost always find something unique in their pictures. As I took their picture out to be framed, I would often point out a little bird, bunny, or other interesting pattern that I could see in their painting. They were always thrilled.

Ellie and I lived happily for a while. We didn't make much money, but we were kind of able to support ourselves. I remember going to a restaurant for lunch and splitting a hamburger as our only meal of the day. Other days, I would get one slice of pizza before my afternoon work schedule began. I remember taking late-afternoon naps on the beach after working the day shift. Nights we walked the boardwalk with our guitars, meeting people in groups for impromptu gatherings and singing.

It was free and fun, and we were both very young and pure—not into drugs, drinking, or sex. We were happy. But being young girls, we were also fickle, meaning we got bored easily.

Tony lived in the other room over the bar, and we didn't know much about him. One of the few things I remember was that he always blocked his eyes with his hand if he came into our room and we were in our pajamas or not sufficiently dressed. He often knocked on our door to ask if one of his girlfriends could use our bathroom. We always said yes, because his space had no facilities. We saw a wide variety of his female guests.

The other thing I remember about Tony is that he gave us a whole roll of red tickets to use on the boardwalk rides. This was such an exciting gift, because we loved rides but didn't have the money to buy tickets. His only stipulation was to be sure to tell anyone who asked about these tickets that we had just found them. We agreed, and we were off!

We rode on all of our favorites, especially the helicopter patrol, which is still my favorite. It was a sideways Ferris wheel that went over the ocean. It felt like flying! But our adventure didn't last as long as we had wished. We were on a train ride when suddenly, we were being pointed out and asked to leave. During the questioning of where we got these red tickets, we repeated our promised lie that we had just found them. I was so frightened that I could feel my mouth turning dry, my heart pounding, and this horrible sinking feeling in my stomach. We were dismissed with a severe warning not to return.

Another adventure came when my friend, who used to work at Skee-Ball, asked me to do him a favor. He had "acquired" some prize tickets and wanted to get a few things. As a thanks for cashing in the tickets, he said that I could choose something for myself. I didn't have the sense to realize that this was not the right thing to do, so I did it.

I do not remember what I picked up for him, but I do remember choosing a huge, hot pink stuffed animal for myself. I was delighted, as I had never owned such a thing, but I was not delighted to realize that the manager had followed me out of the store and around the corner to where my "friend" was waiting for his loot.

The manager took one look at his ex-employee, and a loud discussion ensued. All I remember was arguing with the man very loudly for myself, and I clearly remember him saying that I could keep the stuffed animal but warning, "One day, your mouth is going to get you in trouble."

I did keep that big stuffed cat (or whatever it was) for a while, but I easily gave it away, because it never really gave me any pleasure. I learned that material things earned dishonestly gave me no joy. If anything, they made me feel sad and bad about myself.

Those little brushes with unethical behavior were frightening. I remember walking with Ellie on the beach late that night as I realized that dishonesty was not for me. I made a promise to myself not to do that again, and I have kept that promise to this day.

Lesson Learned

Honesty is the best policy.

Material items acquired illegally or that do not belong to you give no pleasure. If anything, they can drag you down. They are simply not worth having.

Material items can hold energy. If you are unsure about this or are trying to decide whether to keep an item in your possession, hold or touch the item and ask yourself, "Does this item make me feel good or bad? Does it raise or lower my energy? Or is it neutral?"

If you really don't need or use an item that makes you feel sad or low, see if you can find a better place for it—even if that better place is the garbage!

* * *

So our time in Ocean City, Maryland, was growing sour. Not only was the bloom off the rose, but we were feeling scratched up by the thorns. Deciding to try a new adventure, we packed up our sparse belongings, quit our jobs, hopped on a bus, and tried our luck back in Atlantic City, where I had stayed the summer before.

The night before our departure, something very serendipitous happened to me. We had a very large male friend who was a judo master. He insisted on taking me out to the beach to teach me some self-defense moves. I agreed, and we had a mini lesson. The only thing he taught me that I still remember is that if a man ever threw me down, I should bend my legs up and be ready to kick like hell. He made me practice this over and over.

The next day, we took the bus to Atlantic City and found housing in my old coed rooming house. We had a room with a sink, and we shared the one women's bathroom with the rest of the hall. Because it was in the middle of the summer, many jobs were already filled. However, we found simple waitress jobs in a rooming house for older people who came for extended stays to enjoy the beach atmosphere.

The meals were served in a communal dining room. All the guests had assigned tables, and we would have the same clients for weeks.

We wouldn't get a tip until they left. I remember that two red-haired fellows from Ireland also worked there. They were speaking our same language, but their accents and colloquialisms were unique. I loved to listen to them, and they made me smile.

The other thing I remember is that at one of my tables, there was a blind man and his wife. They were visiting for the entire summer. It made such an impression upon me that even though the man was blind, when he got up, he always pushed in his chair. My feeling was that if a person with a disability can do the proper thing, so could I. Later, I came to realize that blind people rely on things being in their proper place. From that day forward, whenever I get up from a table in a restaurant, I always push in my chair.

On one occasion, when Ellie and I were in the lobby of our rooming house and returning to our room, a large, burly bully of a man grabbed Ellie's arm and started dragging her toward the stairs. He had long, dark, stringy hair, and he was muscular with plenty of extra stuffing. Compared to us, he was huge! She tried to resist, but being a frail little thing, she was no match for his apelike muscles.

Without thinking, I grabbed his other arm and started pulling on him while yelling, "Leave her alone!"

He turned to look at the distraction and said, "OK, then I'll take you!" Without much effort, he started pulling me up the stairs. Ellie tried to help, but to no avail.

He quickly pulled me with full force down the hall and then into his room. He slammed the door shut, and it locked automatically. I could hear Ellie pounding on the outside of the door. I think he was quite drunk or drugged.

I remember that he immediately threw me on the bed, and then he started fumbling with his pants. My body reacted automatically, and all that self-defense practice on the beach paid off. My knees went up toward my head, and when he started to come down on me, I kicked with all my strength, which threw that huge ape man (who was at least twice my weight) across the room. I remember the sound of the thud as he landed against the wall and started groaning in pain.

I jumped up, got out the door, dashed with Ellie into our room, and slammed and locked the door. He came after us, and I remember the huge apelike hands trying to climb through the transom window that was over the door. It had a slanted opening for air.

He couldn't get in, but there were no phones, and we stayed trapped for hours, afraid to come out. Finally, when we did brave a peek out, we saw our sweet, protective Cuban friend. After I told him what had happened, I remember he put his arm around my back, holding my arm securely, and in broken English said, "Don't-ah you worry. I will not let him hurt you. I will-ah punch him out." I was relieved to have his protection.

A day or so after that incident, on the way to our room, as we arrived in our upstairs hallway, we encountered a kangaroo court. Males who lived on the hall were accusing our ape man of raping several of their girlfriends. A friend of his was standing beside Ape Man, swearing that Ape Man was with him the whole time.

We just went quietly into our room. The decision was made, and Ape Man was forced to leave our boardinghouse. We were of course relieved that he was gone, but the seriousness of our experience really sank in.

So how could a five-foot three-inch, weak little teenage girl throw a six foot two-hundred-pound muscleman across a room and survive when so many had not? What forces came together to teach me the one skill that saved me?

Lessons Learned

This is a true story that can also be seen as a metaphor.

We all have secret superpowers inside of us. What happened to me was the familiar fight, flight, or freeze response brought about by our bodies producing adrenaline in emergency situations in order to save our lives.

This survival mechanism has been protecting mankind and womankind since caveman days. It helped us freeze so a bear could not detect us, put blood in our limbs to run like hell away from predators, or in my case, fight like hell when cornered. We all have this quiet superpower. It is a part of our DNA. Once the emergency passes, our bodies are meant to return to a calm state of equilibrium.

It is important for us to reside in a relaxed, centered space, because when we are calm, our bodies have a chance to heal and digest our food. It is in the relaxed state that we have the best access to the problem-solving, intuitive, and logical parts of our brain.

The problem is that in our current society, our survival mechanisms are too often triggered by everyday stresses, like a computer problem, a traffic incident, a fight with loved ones, or a threatening encounter with a boss or other authority figure. We find ourselves in a constant state of stress. This can be a detriment to both our health and our spirit.

There are simple techniques, which I will share, that can be used to return to a calm state. Feeling safe is the first step, and it is essential if we wish to hear our voice of inner wisdom.

In Part Three and Four of this book, I have compiled my favorite ways to calm down, relax, and de-stress. They are tools that you can also use to slow down and begin to tune in to the inner, wiser part of yourself.

2

Thrown Off the School Bus

I REMEMBER WALKING DOWN THE AISLE of the school bus in shame. I felt queasy, dizzy, and weak as I heard the gagging and moaning sounds of the other young passengers. I heard them groaning the *eewh* sound. I was following my furious sister as we walked toward the bus exit.

I had vomited on the school bus, and the bus driver had stopped the bus and was putting us out in the middle of nowhere (to avoid a mass vomiting, I guess). My sister was stomping ahead, asking why *she* had to be part of this shameful debacle.

The story really begins with a crush. His name was Peter, and his locker was right next to mine. Even though I was only in eighth grade, and he was a year or so older, we often exchanged greetings and smiles. I remember the strangest things about him. He had beautiful blue eyes, but the amazing part was that he had the ability to make his irises twirl in a dizzying way. He could do this on demand, which he often did for my enjoyment and amazement.

One Friday afternoon, he asked me, "What are you doing this weekend?"

I really liked him, but I had never been asked out on a date before. I knew he was asking me out, and I panicked. I froze, and then I said the first thing that I could think of: "I'm babysitting."

That was a total lie. I started getting upset and worried. Why had I said that? What could I do?

After lunch, there was a study hall, and Peter and I were both in it. As we were all entering the room and getting settled, some girl said very loudly, "Sandy, I heard you like Peter."

Again, I reacted without thinking. "I do not!" I protested. As soon as it was out of my mouth, I was sorry. The look on Peter's face was devastating.

I started to feel sick, upset, and worried. I worried all through study hall. I was still ruminating and putting myself deeper and deeper into agony through my final period with Miss Bigg's geometry class.

All I could think about was how I had ruined my only chances with Peter and hurt his feelings. I started to feel more and more queasy and sick to my stomach. I literally worried myself sick. I worried and worried and worried, until that dizzy swirling sensation started creeping up. The room started to spin, and I vomited right there in class!

I was sent to the restroom and then to the school nurse, who somehow thought it would be wise to put a child who was vomiting on a bus full of other students. *Wrong!*

For the first part of the bus trip, I was OK, but the nausea soon returned, and the vomiting reoccurred when we were about halfway home. The bus driver stopped the bus and put me off at the only place she could find with a phone. For extra security, she made my older sister, Roz, come with me.

The place we found ourselves was called Old Tavern. It was a bar! I can only imagine what would become of a school bus driver today who kicked a sick student off the bus and left her at a bar, but it was the 1960s, and things were different back then.

Roz went into the establishment to locate a phone and call our father. I remember that she made me wait outside. I guess she didn't want any more embarrassment from me. Daddy came to the rescue and ended our adventure by delivering us safely home.

When we arrived, my grandmother was there, and I remember Mom and everyone being so sympathetic and concerned. "She must have a twenty-four-hour virus or some flu," they said. But I knew I had no virus or flu. I knew in my heart, that I had done this to myself. I had literally made myself sick.

Lessons Learned

First of all, if someone is literally vomiting, it is probably not a good idea for them to get into a moving vehicle.

But most importantly, I discovered that I have an amazing superpower: I can literally make myself sick with my thoughts!

I learned that our thoughts are very powerful, especially when combined with strong emotions.

Have you ever been very upset, and then gotten sick or experienced an unfortunate accident?

As an aside, wouldn't it have been wonderful if, back then, I'd had enough self-esteem to accept a kind boy's warm attention? And wouldn't it have been wonderful if I'd had enough confidence and self-regard to speak my own truth and say, "Yes, of course I like Peter. I think he's grand!" But then I would never have learned the important lesson that day: not to dwell on worry and negativity. Those of us who are very sensitive do not have the prerogative to stay in deep sadness for prolonged periods of time.

Please understand: I am not telling you to ignore your feelings or to put on a fake positive front. If you are an empath, you probably feel everything very deeply. It is important to own, feel, and experience those feelings. Let yourself mourn and cry and be real about what is happening and what you are experiencing. But please, seek help if you get stuck in negativity.

3

Overwhelmed in a Hallway

We were packed together like sardines. It was a large hallway, but we were all smashed together waiting for the double doors to open. We were college freshman on our first important orientation task: to register for our classes. I was unprepared for this survival of the fittest task.

Armed only with a small slip of paper that the guidance counselor had given me as a guide, I struggled in the crowd. We were so tight together that if someone moved, I was shoved and moved. I had no control. There was plenty of movement because some smarter or more aggressive types were struggling to get to the front of the line. It felt hard to breathe.

It was very scary, and I really had even less of an idea of what to do when the double doors finally did open. We were all swept into a large room where professors were standing behind tables. I felt confused and overwhelmed. It took me a little while to figure out that over each of the tables was the name of the class.

I looked at my little piece of paper and saw "English 101." *OK, I thought, I will head over to that table.* But before I could get across the room, there was already a long line at that station.

I patiently waited in line, but when I reached the end of the wait, the class was already filled. I searched for another class and another line, but it was always the same. It felt as if everyone else had more faculties to manage such chaos. Some people even had researched the best professors to choose.

Finally, as the rest of the people cleared out, I found a few classes that were not filled. The ones that were left were all night classes! So, in my first semester as a college student, I had all night classes. Instead of meeting early in the morning for three days a week, my classes would meet one evening for several hours. So, while everyone in the dorm had to drag themselves out of bed for those ungodly early-morning classes, every morning, I could sleep in.

Lessons Learned

Things have a way of working out for the best.

And, more importantly, I now understand a few things about being a highly sensitive person.

It is easy to get overwhelmed in chaotic situations, and especially in crowded ones.

It is important not to be hard on yourself.

If you are easily overwhelmed, it is most likely that you are like a finely tuned radar device picking up on energy patterns of which others are oblivious. It is similar to a dog who can smell things that most of us humans cannot. Just because others do not perceive something doesn't mean that it does not exist. In a crowd, it is easy for an empath to be overwhelmed by other people's emotions and other problems.

At times, the newly awakened empath can feel a type of overload when confronted by too much commotion. Protect yourself by planning ahead. When you know that certain situations are more difficult for you, see what accommodations you can make for yourself. When planning to approach difficult situations, try to be at your best. Is it better for you to eat and be hydrated? Is it best to enter these situations when you are feeling emotionally and physically stable? Learning to balance your energies is paramount. Go in solidly grounded.

Some people avoid crowds when possible. The most important thing is to not be too hard on yourself when you get overloaded and scrambled. There are specific energy exercises that can really help. My favorite ones are listed in Part Four of this book.

4

Who Does This Belong To?

"**W**HY DO YOU ALWAYS HAVE what I have?"

The question startled me. It came from my nursing-school dorm buddy. We had been close friends through elementary school and high school, then shared an apartment in college, but now we were sharing a small dorm room in our first year as nursing students.

I hadn't really responded, so she asked again, "Why is it that if I have a headache, you have a headache? Why is it that if I have a sinus problem, you say your nose is stopped up? And why did your back start to hurt when I was the one who strained my back?"

At that moment, I had no answers. But this was the very first time I awakened to the idea that not everything I was feeling in my body was mine.

I still am not completely sure exactly why I pick up on some people's physical ailments and not others, but I am starting to understand a few general truths. Being in close proximity seems to be a factor for me. Even though we had been close confidants for years, this was the first time my friend and I had shared a small dorm sleeping space. My desire to help also seems to be an issue. Often, I pick up on a client's energetic patterns before, during, or after their sessions. The more invested I am in the person, the more likely it is that I may mirror them.

My roommate was also my childhood friend, and I loved her dearly. A few years later, when she was in labor with her first child, I found myself squatting on the kitchen floor moaning in agonizing abdominal pain—even though we lived hundreds of miles apart. Thankfully, through the years, I have found some things that have been helpful to me.

Lessons Learned

Not everything we are experiencing physically belongs to us.

If you suspect that you have taken on other people's physical symptoms, the first step is to recognize what is yours and what is not. One way to determine this is to simply ask, *Who does this belong to?* Listen for an answer. It is amazing what answers you will get if you breathe, center yourself, and ask.

Once you know that a physical pain or sensation does not belong to you, my favorite thing to do is to sing to myself a phrase from an old Elvis Presley song. It is merely, "Return to Sender." I include the next line, "address unknown, no such number, no such phone." In my mind, I imagine the energetic letter getting lost on the way back.

Sometimes it may not feel good to send a symptom back to a client or a loved one. My energy medicine teachers have encouraged the technique of visualizing the problem draining out of the bottom of the spine and onto the ground. In Silva meditation, we visualize throwing unwanted symptoms into a black hole. The important thing to remember is that other people's physical symptoms don't belong to you. Perhaps they are meant as a lesson or a guidance for the other person. Your suffering with another's problem does not ease that person's pain or help that person in any way.

After singing my little Elvis song to myself, I thank my body for letting me know about the problem. (Realize what an incredible superpower this is!) I say to myself *I no longer need this*. I trace figure-eight patterns over the pain or uncomfortable place on my body, or just off of my body, in the field or aura.

Usually, I do both while repeating something like *I release anything that is not love or light*, or *I release anything that does not serve me*, or *I let go of anything that doesn't belong to me*, or *It is safe to let this go*. The exact words are not important. Say whatever feels right to you. The important thing is to be willing to let it go. Often, taking a shower or bath helps. (I find that sea salt baths are particularly helpful.)

Preventive and other helpful strategies include drinking enough water, getting enough rest, eating the proper diet for your body, getting fresh air and exercise outside near nature, and using grounding and other energy balancing techniques. You are much more likely to be thrown off balance if you are already unsteady from sugar crashes, stress, and exhaustion. Keeping your own energies balanced and especially grounded is essential! I use techniques that I have learned from Silva and Donna Eden. These resources and techniques are listed in the back of this book.

Notes

- The reason crossover or figure-eight patterns are helpful is that they balance energies and release pain. We have crossover patterns all over our body, down to our DNA. The left hemisphere of the brain controls the right side of the body, and the right hemisphere controls the left side. We have several crossover stations in the head that similarly affect the eyes and ears.
- The idea to ask myself "Who does this belong to?" and then return the ailment back to sender I learned from listening to Dain Heer of Access Consciousness. I adjusted and added to the idea to make it work better for me. For more information on Dr. Dain Heer, check out the suggested reading list in the back of this book.

5

Love in an Elevator

As I entered the ancient hospital and dashed toward the closing elevator door, I yelled, "Hold the elevator!"

That darn elevator! It took forever, and here I was just missing it. I couldn't believe I would have to stand for endless upon endless minutes waiting for it to go all the way up to the top floor and then back down again. Hadn't it been a long-enough day?

I was in my third year of college and my first year of nursing school. I'd already had a full day of classes and labs and on-the-floor training. I was in tan jeans with a yellow shirt peeking out of my white lab coat. My tortoiseshell glasses were perched on my nose, and just for the hippy touch, yellow shoelaces adorned my tan shoes.

I needed to get to the tenth floor to meet and get acquainted with the patient who would be mine tomorrow. I'd had a lonely dinner in the dining hall and an interesting intuition on the walk over to the hospital. Some little voice in my head said, *You are going to meet someone tonight.*

That was not at all in my mind as I rushed toward the extremely crowded elevator and saw the doors closing. I felt pure impatience, exasperation, and frustration. I had missed that elevator merely by seconds!

Then suddenly, the door was not closing—it was opening! I ran and squeezed in. There was no real way to turn around even if I knew the proper elevator etiquette, which I didn't; I was a small-town Virginia country girl, from a town called Marshall, with a population of 500 people; (499, since I was now a nursing student at the prestigious Medical College of Virginia, in the big city of Richmond.)

We didn't have elevators in Marshall, so there was no way I could have known that it is customary to turn around and face the door, not stare straight into the eyes of a complete stranger who, unbeknownst to me, was the knight in shining armor who had put his foot in the door.

We rode up ten floors just staring into each other's faces. It was easy, because he was five foot six, very close to my height of five foot three and a half. There was just enough in those few inches for me to look up into his eyes.

But whoops! In just a moment, we were on the tenth floor, the maternity wing—my stop. I went to step out but glanced back at that cute guy. He winked at me! I smiled, sighed, and then went in search of my patient.

I never met her or found her, so I was back at the nursing station looking over charts when I looked up to see the elevator doors opening. There was that cute guy again on another crowded elevator. He waved at me as the elevator doors closed. *That's interesting*, I thought as I smiled to myself.

I was still at the nurse's station going over charts when I looked up to see that same young man, with intriguing hazel eyes and dark soft curly hair, standing beside me. He merely said, "I just had to come back."

I said, "I'm glad you did."

I left the charts and took his hand, and we found the stairwell. We ran down ten flights of stairs laughing and holding hands.

We sat outside on the grass under a tree trying to understand why we both felt as if we knew each other. We recognized each other right away, but we didn't know why or how. So we went over our entire lives, step by step, to see if ever our paths had crossed. He was from Livingston, New Jersey. He had been traveling around the country after graduating from Pitt.

Was it Woodstock? No, I didn't go; I was still in high school at that time, and while my parents let me do a lot, they wouldn't let me go to a hippie music festival. Was it a Jewish summer camp or convention?

No, we were in different ones. Summers at the beach? No, we didn't go to the same beaches.

We never have been able to figure it out! But there was such a tremendous pull that neither of us could ignore it. As we were talking, I noticed that he had added purple shoelaces—my favorite color!

His story was that he had heard and seen me running and yelling "Hold the elevator," so he put his foot in the door. In his words, "I saw this girl, and she was *really* cute." He was the one who had forced the closing door to reopen. He'd had the same experience as we gazed into each other's eyes. But after I got off, he went to find a hospitalized friend on an upper floor. When he couldn't find the friend, he got back on the elevator and rode to the ground floor.

A voice started calling to him, *Go back and find that girl.*

Ridiculous, he thought to himself. *I'll never find her, and besides, what on earth would I do if I did?*

He walked slowly down the street back to his little yellow pickup truck, but he couldn't just get in and drive away. He headed back to the hospital. He thought, *I don't even know what floor she is on! This is ridiculous! I don't do such things!* So he turned around and headed back to his truck again.

Then a voice overtook him. It said, *If you don't go back and find that girl, you will regret it for the rest of your life.*

He marched back to the elevator. When he got on, it was full of people. He pushed every button, which annoyed everyone there. He was searching for something familiar on each floor, to find something he might recognize. Instead, he actually saw the girl he was looking for.

Now he knew that it was the tenth floor, but the elevator was going up. He stayed on, and then pressed the tenth-floor button on the way back down. When the doors opened on the tenth floor, he took a deep breath, decided to take a chance, bravely stepped out of the elevator, and courageously approached.

The rest is history. As of this writing, we are approaching our forty-fifth wedding anniversary. We have a son and a wonderful daughter-in-law, and two beautiful granddaughters.

This true, serendipitous meeting happened in a matter of seconds. I could easily have missed that elevator. What brought both of us to that place at that very moment? Why couldn't I find my patient, and why couldn't he find his friend?

Lessons Learned

Always listen to the voice of your higher self. It is your inner guidance and always there when you learn to listen.

The first step to hearing your own guidance is to learn to center yourself. Take a breath, ask, and then listen. What you are meant to do makes you feel lighter. If it is a flow, it is a go.

When you think you want to do something, and you find obstacles after obstacles in your way, reconsider. Go through doors that are open. Don't stubbornly knock your head against closed doors. When it's not a flow … let it go.

6

Choking in a Fancy Restaurant

Jeff and I were treating ourselves to a very fancy French restaurant. I don't remember the occasion or reason for such a big splurge, but because of our experience, we have never seemed to ever go to a fancy French restaurant again. I started feeling as if something was horribly wrong with my father. A sick choking sensation was overtaking me.

My dad was in Virginia where I grew up, and we were living in Atlanta, Georgia. Jeff was working for the Oleg Cassini sports clothes division of a company named Munsingwear, a large clothing manufacturer. The company had packed us up and moved us from our New Jersey apartment when it opened an Atlanta branch.

Moving from the cold, dark, dreary snows on February first to the bright Atlanta sunshine of almost spring was so wonderful. We both felt so free as we started the next chapter of our lives together. We opened a bank account together and excitedly signed the lease for our sweet little apartment in Stone Mountain, Georgia.

Everything seemed easier there. Everything was on one floor, even our own little washer and dryer. There were lovely places in our apartment complex to walk around, including a lake that overlooked the famous Stone Mountain.

Friends and opportunities came as easily as the beautiful spring weather. We spotted one such opportunity as we drove on a busy highway nearby. There was a big black and white sign that said *Mind Control*. We were so intrigued that we found ourselves turning our little truck around to investigate.

It turned out to be Silva Mind Control, which is now called the Silva Method, so as to be more politically correct. After all, no one wants someone else to use mind control on them. However, that is *not* what Silva is about. It is a beautiful meditation technique that one can learn to center oneself in order to be more open to one's own inner guidance.

We signed up for the course and found ourselves in classes in a large room with like-minded people. We learned to relax, meditate, and start listening to our intuition.

So, we were open when I started receiving a strong intuitive message. The fancy restaurant food was a little too fancy. We were among the only patrons there, so the service was excellent, but actually *too* excellent. Jeff was a smoker back then, and every single time he flicked an ash into the ashtray, a waiter came to take it away and give him a clean one. He was getting annoyed anyway, so when some strange thing came over me, he was ready to leave.

A horrible feeling was overtaking me. I started feeling as if my father was choking and unable to breathe. I had feelings in my throat and my solar plexus. It felt like a huge dark cloud of upset. I became very emotional, as if I had just heard the worst kind of news. I felt as if I could burst out in tears of grief, because I knew something was terribly wrong with my daddy.

Jeff, being the always-supportive love that he is, took me seriously. Back then, there were no cell phones, so we quickly left the restaurant to drive to our apartment to call. My voice was shaky when I heard my mother's voice and asked, "Is Daddy OK?"

I was shocked when she said he was fine, but then she always said that. I asked to speak with him anyway.

I started questioning him, and he said, "I'm OK, but I'm very shook up. We were just on a rescue squad call. A young man drowned in a lake. We tried and tried, but we couldn't resuscitate him. It was very upsetting."

Sandy Westerman

Lessons Learned

We can pick up feelings and emotions that do not belong to us. It wasn't but a few months later when Dad got a very serious diagnosis of pancreatic and liver cancer.

7

A Deathbed Promise

January 30, 1975

Daddy was only fifty-eight and dying. It was late at night and my turn to sit beside his hospital bed while Mom got a little sleep in a nearby vacant room.

It had been eighteen long months since Daddy's initial pancreatic and liver cancer diagnosis. It was discovered after months of pain, leading to an exploratory gall bladder operation. Back then, there were no scans to check things out.

Dad had searched for anything that would cure him, and so had I. He tried chemotherapy, and I searched under every rock for alternatives. There were no internet searches back then.

I was a nurse, but I was seeking a more spiritual solution. Jeff and I were in the Silva course, which opened up a myriad of other amazing options. We explored everything that we could find.

We discovered Dr. O. Carl Simonton. He was an oncologist who was combining radiology with Silva-type visual imagery meditations with his patients. It was the mid-seventies and the birth of the mind-body connection. He combined his treatment with positive support groups and was having excellent results.

I got his books and tapes and taught my dad. It gave him great comfort and probably extended the length and quality of his life. Back then, it was seldom that a patient with a metastatic pancreatic cancer diagnosis lived beyond six months. It also brought us closer together.

We had many lovely conversations, not the least of which were about his feelings about dying. He said, "I'm not afraid of dying. I am just afraid and worried about how everyone will manage without me." So, there were promises made.

He made my younger brother, Michael, promise to always take care of Mama. (He was a young man, barely out of high school.) He made Jeff promise that he would always take care of me, and then he worried and worried about my older unattached sister, Roz. Back then, it was thought that women needed men to protect and care for them. Even back then, though, my sis was confidently capable of taking care of herself!

Everyone promised things *to* him—except me. I made him promise something to *me*. Jeff and I were to be married the upcoming weekend. We had rushed together a small family gathering so that my beloved father could be there to see me married. But he was in a coma after a botched, ill-advised surgery to reattach his bowel around an inoperable tumor. It was supposed to give him relief and more time, but all it was doing was giving him tremendous pain and less time. He had been comatose ever since the surgery several days before.

I got a strong message in my meditation that said, *Stop the morphine!* Morphine? Who knew he was on morphine? I asked his nurse, and sure enough—the reason he wasn't waking up after surgery was that he was highly drugged.

They stopped it at my command. He woke up, asking, "Why is everybody here?" His sister, Aunt Edna, and my mother's brother, Uncle Abe, had been called in from Harrisburg and Baltimore. It gave the whole family a chance to visit with him one last time.

I told him, "Dad, you've been very sick." I was so angry when I heard my uncle and aunt planning his funeral in the hospital cafeteria with Mom. He wasn't going to die! We were going to use our meditation and positive prayers and thoughts to heal him! How dare they! And on top of that, Jeff and I were to be married in a few days!

Once Dad was awake, I said, "Remember, I'm getting married on

Saturday night. Remember, you promised to be there!" He promised that he would. But unfortunately, his body had different plans.

As I sat beside his bed on the last night of his life, I witnessed the most amazing and beautiful things. He started drifting in and out of his body. He suddenly woke out of a sleeping daze to ask excitedly, "Did you see that? It was so beautiful! No, I guess you didn't see it."

"What was it, Dad? Tell me about it!" I pleaded.

"It was so beautiful!" His whole being was lit up in ecstasy. "It was an amazing white, flying horse with beautiful wings." He described an awe-inspiring sky with lovely clouds.

Oh, how I wished that I could have seen it too, but I was able to feel and sense the joy and peace that it brought him.

It was late at night. To keep my hands busy while I was keeping him company, I was finishing a wool shawl that I had crocheted. The finishing touch was the dark brown contrasting fringe that I was cutting and securing all around it.

Dad was lying flat on his back. He was staring at the ceiling and unable to move or see beyond his upward gaze. Then, unexpectedly, he asked, "What's that all over the floor? What's that brown stuff all over the floor?"

The light was dim. However, as I leaned over to glance at the floor beside my chair, I laughed when I saw all the lost little pieces of dark brown fringe that I had been cutting. What a little mess I was unknowingly making!

"Oh, Dad, that's just the yarn from the fringe I've been working on. Sorry, I didn't realize that I was making such a mess. I'll clean it up."

As I started to clean up the little piles of yarn, he said, "I saw it, but I didn't see it." I knew what he meant. It was impossible for him to have seen it with his eyes, although somehow, he saw it.

I didn't know what to say at the time. Was he starting to leave his body and so floating above at a vantage point that would enable such a vision?

A little time went by. It had been a long night. A sweet nurse came in and asked if Dad would like some apple juice. He declined. However, I was thrilled when she offered it to me. I accepted happily. As I used the straw and felt the cold juice hitting the back my throat, I felt the refreshing energy blast the sweetness was giving my tired body.

Dad piped up again. I thought he had been sleeping, but he very quizzically asked, "Why am I drinking apple juice when I am not drinking apple juice?"

Somehow, through all that sleepiness, I knew what to say. "Oh, I'm the one drinking apple juice, Dad. You are just being especially perceptive."

He seemed content with that response, and I felt how privileged I was to be there to experience that last night with him. It was such a precious time, and I have been forever grateful that I have those memories to cherish.

A little while later, he started feeling more pain than he could bear. That is when he made the decision, his last decision, to take the morphine again. The pain left, and so did his consciousness. It was early morning and he remained in a coma until dawn on the morning of New Year's Eve, when my mom awoke to continue her vigil with him.

Mom had been in the room with us for about an hour when suddenly, I got this edgy feeling that I just had to leave. I felt as if I was crawling out of my skin when I said, "I've just gotta get out of here. I'm going to go call Jeff to tell him to come pick me up."

There were no cell phones back then, so I was getting up to make a call when Dad took his last breath. We take so many breaths in our lifetime. I wonder, why do we always remember the last?

Mom sent me out of the room to get a nurse. When help arrived with me, all I wanted to do was start crying and pounding on his chest, screaming, "Don't die, Daddy." That is what I wanted to do, but I didn't. The sweet nurse literally wrapped me in her arms and escorted us to a quiet room. Mom was following behind.

Mom took a deep breath and said, "I have a wonderful daughter, Roz." I heard her inhale deeply again as she repeated, "I have a wonderful daughter, Sandy," and then again, instead of breaking down, she repeated her deep breathing with the same gratitude for my brother. That was my mother!

Lessons Learned

My mother was very stoic. She didn't really understand the strong emotions that flooded through my body at times. It wasn't for lack of caring. She was married to my dad at the tender age of nineteen. He was the love of her life. She nursed and fed and cared for him tirelessly during his illness.

She was *always* so grateful for anything and everything that she had. She didn't dwell on what she didn't have.

That has been such a good lesson.

Concentrate and be thankful, for what you have, not on what you don't have. If you get nothing out of this book but one thing, please let it be this: *Gratitude changes everything!*

Gratitude is the most powerful thing that you can have to help yourself and improve your circumstances. Be thankful for every little thing and every big thing.

Can you walk? Can you see? Can you hear? Can you breathe comfortably? Do you have loved ones? A roof over your head? A pet? Do you have enough food? A vehicle? A comfortable bed? Clothes? Books? A phone? A computer. You amplify and increase the things you concentrate on with your gratitude. The universe will send more of the same to you. Concentrate on all the blessings that you do have! You have more to be thankful for than you realize.

Notes

The funeral in Baltimore was an endless line of relatives and well-wishers. Instead of a wedding that Saturday night, we were at a memorial service for my dad presented by the town of Marshall (specifically the rescue squad). Not only had Dad helped to establish the squad, but he had been one of the main teachers and trainers for the next generation. He often took emergency calls to help others.

With my father gone, there was no rush for the wedding. But the rabbi was perturbed. He said, "Life should not be put off for death," and besides, we already had the marriage license. I was insistent that we wait until spring, when we could have everyone there and have a big celebration. That is what we did, and that is why our marriage license has a December or January date even though we were married in May.

8

A Poem

January 23, 1976

I WROTE THIS POEM ABOUT THREE weeks after my father's death. I was recalling my emotions, staring out the high hospital window that early dawn morning just before he passed. It depicts the severe grief state of mind that I was experiencing.

Sandy Westerman

Oh death, how slowly you creep up on us.
Gradually, as the morning peeps its head over the crispy frozen trees,
in oranges and reds, and tears,
How lonely you make me feel.
How slowly you bring your relief from pain.
How empty you make me feel, oh death.

You creep up on us, crawling, welcomed though hated.
How cruel you are to take my only father.
How cruel you are to make him wait.
How right you are, how wrong you are,
How lonely I am.

How helpless I feel
Staring out this window at something up high,
But it's nothing,
For you are leaving me.
And I know you have to go, Dad.
But please! Please! Don't leave me!
Don't leave me here!

9

Babbling Psychosis

Even though I had taken a few weeks off work between Dad's illness and death, I wasn't really ready to return to my job. So when I walked through the doorway to the hospital, I was still especially raw and vulnerable. My father and his death were in the forefront of my mind. I still felt very preoccupied and upset, and not really ready to resume my duties as a psychiatric nurse. But there I was anyway.

As I walked in, the first thing I noticed was a woman sitting in the lobby, babbling very loudly. She was a patient waiting for a psychiatric evaluation, and she was endlessly speaking in an incoherent, unintelligible jabber. Her streams of thought were nonsensical to me. She had what we called *loose associations*. That means that everything she becomes aware of just broke into her speech, with no rhyme or reason.

Her litany continued until I walked in a path directly in front of her, and then suddenly she wasn't talking nonsensically at all. She was literally reading my mind and repeating out loud every thought that I was stressing over.

She was loudly, clearly projecting: "My father died! I feel so sad. He was so sick and now he's gone. I don't know how I can face this day. Everything is different now. I don't know what to do! I feel so awful that I feel sick!"

I quickly walked past her, and her subject matter changed. I dashed through the double doors for staff only. Whew! I took a deep breath!

What was that? I kept it completely secret at work. Did anyone else hear that? I started to ask myself, *What is the difference between* psychic *and* psychotic?

Lessons Learned

When some empaths get extremely emotional or upset, they have the ability to put out what Jeff and I call a *very heavy set* (of vibrations). Those strong energetic patterns are easily picked up by sensitive beings in our close proximity. The amazing thing is that people who are emotionally close to us may feel our strong vibes from hundreds of miles away.

How many times have you felt that you just had to call a loved one when that person came into your thoughts out of the blue? How many times has a loved one just known when to call you? We are all connected. It is easier to be receptive to these energetic vibrations when we have our antenna up. We do that when we are centered and in a calm, loving state. When you are in the middle of your own storm, the signals have a harder time getting through.

Regarding my *psychic* versus *psychotic* question, I decided that the answer lies in the ability for one to determine what is really in front of one versus what one is perceiving in one's own mind. In psychosis, a person cannot discriminate reality from imagination. Their delusions are real to them.

10

A Deer Miss

It was a dark, moonless night. We were driving on a winding two-way country road in Virginia. My brother Michael was driving, and Jeff, Roz, and I were scrunched in the back seat. My head was leaned against the cool, hard glass window.

It wasn't important or memorable where we had been or where we were going. It was late, and I was getting sleepy. As I felt myself starting to nod off to sleep, a most unusual thing happened. I heard my inner guide speak to me loudly and clearly. She said, *Take your head off the window. There is going to be an accident, but everything is going to be OK.*

I lifted my head off the window, wondering what the heck had just happened, when suddenly a deer jumped in front of our speeding car. My brother, having excellent reflexes, swerved the car right and left several times, which left us in the back seat jolted back and forth. The fear in the car was palpable, but I remember being very calm, as I heard my own voice clearly saying, *It's going to be OK.*

We avoided a collision with the deer, and with a sigh of relief, we safely continued our journey. No one was injured during the jolting ride, but I surely would have been if my head had remained on the hard glass window.

Lessons Learned

I had been practicing a type of meditation that is taught in the Silva Method. Through breathing and visualization, I had practiced relaxing my body and thoughts. One exercise I use to this day is to visualize a stairway leading to a door. As you count down twelve steps and visualize yourself walking step by step closer to the door, you learn to deeply relax and slow the brainwaves.

As the door magically opens and you visualize yourself in what we call our *workshop*, we feel a deep delicious peace overcome us. This is our safe place, with four walls and a ceiling.

Our special guides are there to advise us, and this is where my female guide has always resided. However, this was the first time that she had ever broken the consciousness barrier and that I had actually heard her voice. The space between waking and sleep is very similar to meditative brain activity. It is called *alpha*.

This experience was awe-inspiring to me. It all happened in my mind, so nobody knew that I had received an amazing protective message, but *I* did!

11

Code Strong

I WAS LYING ON THE FLOOR in the psychiatric unit hallway. I could feel the scratchy carpet beneath my body. A patient was sitting next to me holding my hand for comfort. My stomach hurt, and I couldn't get up. It felt as if things were swirling around my head. I couldn't think straight, but I did know that this is not where I, the charge nurse, should be.

I heard the unit manager yelling "Code strong!" That is what we were trained to do in emergencies when violence had overtaken a situation. That command over the hospital paging system would bring all the security and strong able-bodied people from all around the hospital to the rescue. Unfortunately, the panicked young secretary was just yelling it as she ran down the hallway, which only added to the confusion.

I was injured after having been violently kicked in the stomach. It was the 1970s, and I was working as an RN in an inpatient psychiatric unit in Arlington, Virginia. It was the evening shift, and I was the charge nurse, which meant I was supposed to be in charge. But I wasn't.

This was one of the first times doctors were attempting sex-change operations (or gender reassignment, as it is called today), and on the unit we had a woman in her twenties who had recently gone through the procedure. She had been a six-foot-two, strapping, masculine man, so her body and muscles resembled those of an athlete.

The problem started over a violent incident in the TV room. She had been acting out violently toward the furniture, so the aide, Neil, tried to subdue her. We were trying to get her to the quiet room, which was a padded room, because that was protocol. She was escalating, and we didn't want anyone to get hurt. When I came onto the scene, I saw that she was arguing with Neil and another male aide.

Even though I had a pretty good relationship with her, don't ask me why I got in the way. The two aides had her by the arms, and they were trying to forcefully take her to seclusion, but they were no real match for her brute strength. I stupidly tried to reason with her, and she kicked out with all her strength, hitting me in the gut, knocking the wind out of me and my feet out from under my body.

When I hit the floor, she got frightened and quickly let the aides take her to seclusion, with no more resistance. I remember watching that from my vantage point flat on my back on the floor.

I don't remember how they got me to the emergency department, but I do remember being on a stretcher when they wheeled me in. The doctors were joking with me that I had been awarded the Rocky fighting award for the night. They checked me out thoroughly, and nothing was broken or injured. I just suddenly knew what it meant to have the shit kicked out of you, literally.

When Jeff arrived, he was furious. He wanted me to quit that job immediately. I took several days off to recover physically and emotionally. When I returned, the kicker's psychiatrist talked with me. I couldn't believe that the young woman had kicked me on purpose, and apparently, she hadn't. She had been questioned as to why she would kick a small petite young female. Was she jealous because she still had such a masculine body?

Her response was very clear. She said, "I wasn't trying to kick Sandy. I was aiming for Neil's balls." I felt a little better knowing that it was sort of an accident.

Lessons Learned

First of all, I have no physical strength or training in martial arts or self-protection. I have never done anything athletic. As much as I thought I was trying to be of some help in controlling an out-of-control person, I had no power to do so. I should have stayed back, out of the way.

Secondly, this was a crazy stressful job. It was so difficult for me to work there and be exposed to so much emotional upheaval. There were so many rules and stresses put on the staff to follow specific protocols within certain time frames. For breaches, we were questioned and severely chastised.

It was no place for a sensitive empath. At times, the staff was crazier than the patients. Several of the psychiatrists had had inappropriate relationships with patients. We had to deal with violence, suicide, mania, and depression daily. We were required to use outdated procedures on patients. The head nurse was so crazy and unreasonable that most of the staff had already resigned.

For some reason, I didn't know how to let go. Every night, I would come home stressed and upset. That head nurse was so out of control that she was eventually fired.

There are nudges we get from the universe when we need to make changes in our lives. If we do not get the gentle messages, we get a literal kick. It is not wise to stay in situations where you are dreadfully unhappy. There is always a choice. There are always options. Sometimes we have to think outside of the box and be brave enough to stand up for ourselves and make changes.

12

Wedding Visit

May 14, 1976

It was the night before our wedding, and I couldn't sleep.

It had been a busy day. Jeff and I had tried to run our wedding rehearsal on our own, with no elder guidance or idea of what we were doing. Even though we knew what we wanted, our siblings and other participants had their own ideas and were at times less than cooperative.

No matter; we gave in a little and got back to the house for a delicious Friday evening rehearsal dinner that Mom had prepared entirely on her own. There were so many people that we had to set up the entire living room with long tables. Never before or after had that ever happened.

I was too excited to notice my dear sweet mother. It had only been five short months since Dad's passing, and here she was trying to handle all of this entirely on her own. It was such a financial issue that both my brother and sister's wedding gifts to us were helping to pay for the wedding.

If I have any regrets, it would have been that some of us would have at least helped her clean up that night. But I was the bride to be and, as many young people are, lost in the excitement of my own world. It was so much the case that I couldn't sleep that night. I felt a strong calling coming from deep inside my soul. I went downstairs and out to the side porch. A breeze was blowing off the adjacent woods, and I was craving the sweet fresh air.

I was pulled to our old metal rocking chair, and as I approached, feelings of my father started to overtake me. As I let myself sink into the ancient metal rocking chair, I felt as if I was melding into, and sitting down into, my father's spirit. It was as if our energies were merging, and we were becoming one.

I allowed myself to sink deeply into a meditative state in order to experience it fully. I could clearly hear his voice asking me, *Why wasn't there a place for me to sit at the rehearsal dinner?*

I was shocked! How could this be happening? I had never ever heard of someone not knowing that they had passed, but certainly this was what was happening here. I'd never experienced this type of other side communication before, but somehow, I knew what to do. I calmly replied, "Dad, you died."

I spent a little while with him, guiding him toward the light. It was an amazing experience for me, but only the first of many times that I have answered the call to aid a friend or family member on the other side. I'd never heard of anyone else who experienced such things, so I mostly kept it to myself.

Through the years, many of my loved ones on the other side would stick around a little while to help me with the next souls, who might be having a more confusing or challenging time. I received many spiritual gifts and insights doing this work, and it always leaves me feeling uplifted.

The next day, just before I walked down the aisle, I panicked and almost started to cry. "I can't!" I said, "I can't do it without Daddy." I had wanted to walk down the aisle alone because I felt that there was no replacement for my father. I had planned to wear and hold on to his gold ring as I walked down the aisle, but now I was panicking.

My very dear, practical brother piped up in the nick of time. All he said was, "He's here with you." That was enough to calm me down and remind me of the truth: that his spirit was with me.

The photographer was very upset with all the photographs of me walking down the aisle. Every single one had me walking to the side with a glowing ball of white light over my right shoulder. He blamed it on other flashes and reflections and a myriad of other excuses. He was disappointed with his work, but we weren't. It was such a clear visual representative of how I was feeling Dad's presence as the two of us walked together down the aisle.

Lessons Learned

Be aware of any promises made on a deathbed.

They are forever.

I had forgotten that on the last night of my father's life, I had made him promise to come to my wedding. But *he* hadn't! He was fulfilling his promise.

It has been said that parents open the gates of heaven for us. In my case, this has literally been true. With every passing, there has been a type of gift.

And on another note, brides and grooms always think it's all about them, when actually, a wedding is a ceremony for both of the families. It is an important life passage for everyone. Let elders guide you with advice about who to invite and the usual customs. Rituals can be very soothing and beautiful in life-passage situations.

13

Gifts Wrapped Up as Visions from the Future

It is said that pregnant women's dreams and visions are especially intriguing. My experiences left no disappointment on that front. And of the thousands of dreams I have dreamed, the special ones, the precognitive ones, are the ones that never fade away. They remain as clear today as when they first appeared—in this case, forty years ago.

The first experience I will call a vision, for lack of a better word, because nothing I had ever experienced could explain it. It was early morning, and dawn was breaking. I was pregnant and just waking up. It felt as if something had tapped me awake, like a gentle feeling on a breeze. I looked up to see a twirling sphere of energy that resembled a globe with moving circular lines that looked like black atoms swirling all around it.

The magical rotating sphere started in the top corner of the room, where the ceiling meets the wall. It was well within my line of vision, so I was breathlessly able to watch it move along the ceiling/wall line. I thought to myself, *That is my unborn baby's soul*. It felt so special, and a wave of gratitude and awe overtook me. It felt to me as if this was a little check-in visit. I watched, hardly breathing, as it followed the entire ceiling/wall line and then just disappeared through the wall as mysteriously as it had arrived.

I had a strong, calm knowing that surprisingly didn't freak me out or upset me in any way. I knew that no one would understand or believe what I'd experienced, so I have shared this story sparingly.

I drifted back to sleep. However, I never have forgotten those precious moments. I never experienced anything that resembled that again until recently, forty years later.

We were expecting our second granddaughter when again, in the early morning, I was awakened by a magical sphere. It followed the same pattern across the wall/ceiling line. However, this time, the moving, twirling, circular lines were in magnificent colors! Again, I felt certain that I was seeing my granddaughter's soul, checking in with a gentle touch. I felt and appreciated the honor.

While I was pregnant, I had one wonderful precognitive dream. It gifted me with three images, which reminded me of three colored pictures. The first snapshot was of a smiling infant, the second was of a happy toddler pulling up to stand, and the third was of a young, curly-brown-haired, compassionate young man in his twenties, centered and happy and gazing into my eyes lovingly. He had hair on the sides of his cheeks. In those days, men often had what we called *muttonchops*, which was a way to trim their beards leaving something on both sides of their cheeks resembling lamb chops.

Nebbish is a Yiddish word that describes a person who can enter a room and no one would even notice he was there. My son is the complete opposite of that. He is such a high-energy person that when he walks into a room, everyone knows it. He has a strong voice and very high and strong energy. I unknowingly felt that energy during the time I carried him, and so I found myself often unexplainably anxious. This dream was extremely reassuring that everything would turn out well.

We had a frightening and dramatic birth (and few months following) with a premature, sleepless, inconsolable baby. We never saw that first snapshot until late one night not long after we brought him home. Instead of sleeping, I was nursing and comforting and rocking my precious little baby boy. Suddenly, as I lifted him to change our position, he looked into my eyes and gave me that smile, which is the first snapshot and is imbedded in my brain. He looked exactly as I had envisioned, and here he was. Did that mean that the other two pictures would also come true?

Well, they have. The second snapshot, of a happy toddler, I saw many times as he pulled himself up to stand. The last picture very much resembles his college photograph. The muttonchops were replaced by a fully bearded face.

Lessons Learned

What an amazing gift, to be able to be reassured by visions of the future. Have you ever had unexplainable visions, or perhaps a dream that you always remember? Have any of them manifested in the waking world?

> **Note**
>
> Reoccurring dreams, for me, are different and involve dream symbols that are often messages of conflicts that need resolving.

14

Don't Open the Door!

Someone was knocking on the door. With my newborn in my arms, I rushed to open it. I *always* opened the door without hesitation. It was reflexive, after living in a small town where we never even locked the doors. There was no fear or trepidation or even common sense. It was merely habit.

However, this busy morning, as I rushed toward the door, I found myself frozen. It felt like there was a deep field of muddy sludge between me and the door. I felt the sensation in my entire body, and as I tried to reach for the doorknob, I felt as if I couldn't.

It felt so awful and frightening that it stopped me in my tracks. I heard my voice ask, "Who is it?"

A male voice replied from the other side of the protective barrier, "My car broke down in your driveway. Can I come in to use your phone?"

Well, somewhere in my foggy new mama brain, I realized that something was not right. We were currently living not in a small town but in Falls Church, Virginia, a busy suburb of DC. Our driveway was at the end of a guardrail that was on a busy sharp curve. The drive was tucked away, and you really had to be purposefully looking for it to drive in.

I wanted to help this person in distress, but thankfully, I just asked him for a number that I could call for him, while keeping the door securely locked.

I wrote down the number that he gave me, but it was bogus. I called Jeff at work and quickly got through. He was managing a drugstore for a chain called People's. Jeff grew up as a city boy, and he always seemed to know what to do. He said, "Hang up and call the police right now!"

I was on the phone with the police when, suddenly, I heard a loud screeching sound coming from outside. The supposedly broken-down car was speeding away. The knocker's car was apparently fine. He'd had other reasons for wanting access to our house. I had received lifesaving information from my superpower empath ability, even though I didn't know or understand it back then.

Lessons Learned

Always listen and respect your inner knowing.

Apparently, the driver of the car also followed his intuition and was therefore not arrested. Was there ever a time when you felt inner guidance? Did you follow it, or did you just wish that you had?

15

Overpass Collapse

It was an exciting, happy time—one of our first opening weeks of the Healthy Grocer, our very own business. During those practice weeks, Jeff was finding all the bugs that needed correcting before the big grand opening.

Being the early bird that he is, he had been at the store for hours. I was excitedly getting dressed and preparing to drive the short few blocks to join in on the joy and fruits of his many months of hard work. It was his dream come true, and mine too.

I had my keys in hand and was just approaching the door when a wave of fatigue and almost nausea overcame me. Every effort felt excruciating. It was very odd, because I had felt fine just a few minutes before. I really had no choice but to listen to my body, so I gave in, laid down, and took a rest. I actually fell into a deep sleep. It felt almost as if I had been drugged with a magic sleeping potion.

When I awoke, I quickly called Jeff to let him know I was sorry to have taken so long, but that now I really was on my way. His next words stunned me. He said "You better not come! There has been a collapse of the overpass, and your direct route is blocked off. Police and rescue vehicles are there because there was a terrible accident."

There had been construction on the bridge or overpass above the road, and as traffic passed under it, the bridge over the road I needed to travel had collapsed and crushed a car. It killed the unfortunate young woman who happened to be in the car driving under it at that moment. This was shocking news! Had I not gotten that fortunate signal from my body, I could have been driving that exact route, at that exact time.

> **Note**
>
> For months, every time I drove under that overpass, I experienced very uncomfortable feelings of anxiety and panic that seemed to be left over from the tragic accident. I discovered that I was able to avoid absorbing those feelings if I blew out through my mouth in quick short puffs as I drove under. Later, I heard Donna Eden tell us to imagine puffing or pulsing out our energy to prevent absorbing unwanted feelings from others.

Lessons Learned

Listen to the messages you receive from your body.

My body was apparently picking up intuitive signals that my consciousness was unaware of. We don't always understand why things are happening at the time but later discover their merit. It is a good idea to make it a habit to listen, pay attention, and honor what you are feeling.

We are spiritual beings living in a physical body. If we do not take care of that body, where else will we live? If you want to live a happy life, become a loving partner with your body. Rest when you are tired. Give your body good healthy food and water when it needs that. Give it exercise and fresh air to breathe. Follow the signals for elimination and pain.

Avoid being a taskmaster who then turns into a binging rebel to get back for being abused. What does that mean? It means that if you push and push yourself while denying what you really want or need, you may find yourself doing unhealthy, self-destructive things as a type of reward or relief. The slave has to sneak away from the master sometimes.

Wouldn't it be better to be kinder to yourself and work out those destructive patterns?

16

Becoming a Fairy Grandmother

I WAS OVER THE MOON WITH excitement about becoming a grandmother. A friend told me that grandchildren are the rewards you get for not killing your kids. I think that is true, because parenting is always challenging, and it is amazing to have the treasure and gift of a grandchild.

There is a magic when you look into your grandchild's eyes and see something very old, something very familiar, and something fresh and brand new at the same time. You feel as if they are yours, without all the sleepless exhaustive hard work.

When our first granddaughter was in utero, it was very easy for me to have lovely meditative talks with her. She told me that she was coming in for her father and grandfather (Jeff) to help them with their life lessons. She said Mimi, her other grandmother, was to be her mother's support, whereas I was to serve as a spiritual guide, like a fairy godmother for her, my granddaughter. She let me know that we had made a sort of spiritual contract or agreement, and that I was to be there to help her in that way.

When the kids asked us what we wanted our grandparent names to be, Jeff was sure, with a quick, "PopPop for me" response. I wasn't quite sure, so I decided to meditate on it before giving my final answer. After counting down, relaxing, and tuning in, I asked *What should I be called?*

In my mind I heard my granddaughter's little voice reply (with a *don't be silly* tone), *Oh, Nana, you know what your name is.* It is for this reason that I am overjoyed to be called Nana, because she picked it for me.

The most memorable encounter I had with granddaughter #1 before she was born came to me suddenly and unexpectedly. I was driving to our store and was just pulling into a parking spot when I felt my granddaughter's energy coming to me urgently. It was so strong and intense that there was no putting it off. I went with it, staying in the car and closing my eyes to receive the message.

You have to promise that you will help me remember! she said in an urgent tone. *You have to help me remember,* she kept repeating. It felt to me as if she was getting to the point of entering into her body, when one forgets everything from the other side. They forget their mission, their contract, their past experiences, everything. They come in fresh and ready to learn. But here, she seemed so frightened that she would forget her mission.

Remember what? I finally asked. *What do you want me to help you remember?*

She replied simply, *Remember love.*

Lessons Learned

To me, the other side is the same before you come into this physical body as it is after you leave this physical body. When we leave our bodies, we become part of that joyful, beautiful energy. Some call it light, some call it God, and some call it love.

At the time when this episode occurred, I was still writing and directing original musicals for a children's private school. This incident inspired me to write a song called "Remember Love." One of my talented students orchestrated it, and we used it in one of my last shows, in which I conducted a chorus of sixty children singing it.

The message is that no matter what is happening in this physical world, the solution is to rise above it, listen to your heart, and remember love. Remember that we are spiritual beings living in this physical dimension. There is a spiritual solution to all difficulties that we might encounter.

Remember love.

17

Mama

I WAS IN MY PAJAMAS WHEN we got the call. It was after ten at night, and Jeff and I were watching TV. We saw that the call was from the home.

My first response was an ominous feeling of *Uh oh, something's wrong with Mom.* However, I was not prepared for the next words I heard: "I am sorry to tell you that your mother has just passed in her sleep."

What?! I knew that she'd had some issues, but she'd been eating and drinking and perfectly lucid that morning. How could this be?

My body started shaking uncontrollably as I reviewed her health history in my mind. Two months before, a breast lump had been discovered. We tried to get the best diagnosis and treatment that we could without traumatizing her and risking her safety during the COVID pandemic. She was almost ninety-four, with dementia.

I had consulted with my siblings and a naturopath as well as her nurse practitioner and even Mom herself, in a lucid moment. She adamantly opposed going to the hospital for more testing. It was decided to go slowly and holistically, using supplements. Even though her ultrasound showed a solid mass that was most certainly malignant, it was not bothering her at all, and she was not a candidate for aggressive testing or a biopsy, not to mention that we were in the middle of a COVID-19 pandemic, where just entering a hospital could put her at serious risk.

No more was really done except starting her on a supplement cocktail of three powerful antioxidants: grape-seed extract or pycnogenol,

Empath is Not a Four-Letter Word

decaffeinated green-tea extract, and curcumin. We were adding turkey tail mushroom water–based extract and planning on alternating it with reishi mushroom extract after the first month. We'd started slowly, and she had been doing fine for at least a month on the antioxidants and maybe a week or two with the first mushroom extract, but because of her possible diagnosis, I encouraged my brother and sister to come for a visit.

Because of the pandemic, she could have no visitors except at the window. I was alternating FaceTime and window visits, so I was connecting with Mom about twice a week. Plus, there were care plan meetings and other phone calls to keep me updated with staff and doctors about her care.

My brother and sister found it more difficult to connect, because they lived a distance away. It was hard for them to connect via FaceTime because of her dementia, so both of them had planned a window visit.

Jeff and I always brought Cricket, our dog, for our window visits. Mom was always delighted to see us. Activities staff used our phones to do FaceTime at the same time so we could hear each other through the window. Mom was just as delighted to see first my brother, Mike, and then a few weeks later my sister, Roz.

It was almost as if she had waited to see them, because the night of the window visit with my sister, we got a call saying that Mom had unexpectedly thrown up blood.

That was a Monday night. I couldn't have been happier with the home. They immediately started testing and evaluations. Even though she had no fever, and the lung X-ray, COVID test, and urine culture were negative, her white blood cell count was very high and continued to elevate over the upcoming days.

On Wednesday, because she was very nauseated and not eating or drinking, they allowed Jeff and me to visit in person. We had to enter through a special door and be screened. Questions were asked like, "Have you been around anyone who was sick?" and "Do you have a sore throat or have you recently had diarrhea?" and "Have you traveled?"

We passed the interrogation, and our temperatures were checked. Next, we were asked to put on gloves, masks, gowns, and plastic face shields. We were escorted the few steps to her room and told that we were allowed to stay for two hours.

It was then that I got to hug and love up Mom for the first time in eight months, since visiting had been banned. She was up and dressed and sitting in her recliner. I climbed in her lap and hugged her the best that I could with the face shield. She was very nauseated, so I spent the entire time doing energy techniques on her to subdue the nausea. I also concentrated on making FaceTime calls with my sis and brother and a phone call with mom's sister-in-law.

My mother was a very positive person, and one of the only times I ever remember hearing her say "I'm sick!" was when her sister-in-law asked her how she was feeling. Otherwise, Mom would always say, "I'm fine, how are you?"

She didn't eat or drink during our visit, but by Friday morning when I had FaceTime with her, she was drinking water the whole time and munching on crackers. We went over her menu choices for the upcoming week, and she was able to give me clear preferences. I asked if she was hungry for lunch, and she said "Yes!"

I was able to sing the *misheberach*, which is a healing Hebrew prayer. I concentrated on sending healing energy to her with my voice as I played the piano. I asked if she wanted to walk to the dining room for lunch or ride in her wheelchair, and she said, "Walk!"

That was the last time I spoke to her. Apparently, she had eaten lunch and dinner in the dining room that day, then was washed up by her favorite aide and tucked into bed that night. It was only during a routine check an hour and a half later that a nurse discovered that she had passed peacefully in her sleep. From the moment I got the call about her death, my body started to shake.

Note

I have come to realize that often my body starts to shake in response to energy from the other side. This physical reaction often happens before my conscious mind is aware of the connection. It serves as a reminder or trigger for me to tune in.

* * *

I could feel her energy surrounding me like a protective fog. Before I could even choose clothes to put on my body, the Baltimore funeral home was calling, trying to ask about arrangements. From that time on, it was a blur. Things happen very quickly in the Jewish religion. She was buried Monday morning, less than three days after her death.

The initial phone call from the home was such a shock. I found it really hard to figure out what to wear or to make any decisions. Jeff is so amazing. Within minutes, he had the prearranged funeral plans in my hands to discuss with my callers. We were near Harrisburg Pennsylvania, and she had a burial plot next to my father's grave in Baltimore, Maryland. To this day, I am amazed and very thankful about how smoothly everything went.

*   *   *

We were allowed to reenter the nursing home to sit with her body late that night before the undertaker arrived. It was a solemn half hour trip that night. I wasn't sure how I would feel. Dear Jeff was with me the whole way, driving us and then just quietly staying at my side.

We arrived about eleven. The entry was deserted. We were screened and asked to again put on all the personal protective gear. It felt so ridiculous! She was dead! For God's sake! But we complied, and we were walked down the familiar hall like so many times before in those almost four years, but this time, Mama was dead.

As we approached the familiar nurse's station, we were greeted by the staff. One of our favorite aides was in tears. She grabbed me and hugged me (which was completely against pandemic protocol) as she exclaimed, "She was just fine! We washed up and even cleaned her teeth!" Another nurse told how she'd sat with Mom in the dining room just a few short hours before. We approached the room with trepidation. Mom was just quietly lying in bed all tucked in with a stuffed animal.

The same aide had even covered all the mirrors in the room, which is an old Jewish tradition after a death. I later asked the rabbi about that and he said that through the years, many have come up with explanations about not worrying about vanity during Shiva (the mourning period), but the original ancient texts said it was done so that the spirit would not get confused and lost in the mirror.

And speaking of the rabbi, even though it was Shabbos, or Shabbat, or the Jewish Sabbath, and I knew the rabbi wouldn't answer his phone, I took a chance and texted him. He called me right back. I sat on the bed next to Mom, and Jeff was in the recliner. The door was closed, and for that hour from eleven to twelve midnight, we were alone until the rabbi called. What a tremendous comfort he was. We put him on speakerphone and said prayers and songs, as we spoke together quietly. We were ready for the funeral home to come.

The staff gently lifted Mom onto a stretcher using the sheet that was under her body. The charge nurse was alarmed and asked, "Where is her ring?" She always wore a beautiful large opal surrounded by tiny diamonds.

Her aide said, "It fell off her finger, but I put it back on!"

I spoke up and showed them as I lifted my hand, "Don't worry, I have it." I've included this little story to illustrate the detailed, personal, loving care that she was receiving at the nursing home.

Because of the pandemic, not even the funeral home attendant was permitted inside the building. We had to follow the stretcher to the outside door. As we exited the room, I grabbed a few family pictures, thinking that I would be able to return in a week to go through everything else, but I was wrong. That would be my last time in that room. Because of pandemic protocols, everything had to be boxed up by staff, and we had to pick it all up from the entryway later.

We waited a while at the special side door for the people from the local funeral home to come. It was a little after midnight. Finally, one lone young woman arrived. I noticed that her name tag was on upside down, revealing how she had probably left home quickly to answer our call. Again, Mom's body was gently lifted with the sheet onto the funeral home stretcher. The transfer was done outside.

I followed the stretcher as Jeff went for our car. We had to roll the stretcher through the grass, and it was difficult for such a slight soul to push at times. The young woman struggled with a few bumps in the lawn. We arrived at a very regular-looking van, and the slide-in transfer to the makeshift hearse was complete.

The kind young woman did a Namaste-type bow to me before she left. "Take care of yourself," she said as I watched her drive off with what was left in this world of Mama.

Lessons Learned

Little things are big things when done with love.

18

Conversations from the Other Side

The night my mother died, as my head hit the pillow and I was drifting off to sleep, I sensed a warm energetic breeze blowing over my head and face. It felt very familiar; however, there were no words to describe the sensation. It was like a caress of love. It felt like it was from a time in my life before words, a time of being a baby or in the womb.

I knew this energy. It felt like a check-in and a kiss goodnight from my mom. What a gift!

The next few days were extremely busy with funeral arrangements, obituaries, and lots of phone calls. There wasn't a lot of connection with Mom, but when I was able to perceive her, she had some interesting things to say. She first said, *I lived too long.* That statement wasn't really surprising to hear, because it was the kind of thing that we had often heard her say of others.

However, the next part was very lovely to hear: *The good part of living so very long is that so many of your family and loved ones go before you. As hard as all the loss, deep sadness, and grief is to experience, there is that much more joy and celebration and love when you reunite on the other side. It is like a big party! You should come!*

Not now, Mom, I laughed.

During the seven days of mourning, or shiva, we had a candle lit in the kitchen. I could feel Mom's energy around as I sat quietly by myself, called loved ones, and did some reflective reading. There was a protective bubble around me, helping me to forget: forget to eat, forget what I was to be doing, and forget the pain of losing Mama.

But after a few weeks, things changed. I no longer felt Mom's presence, and a deep sadness overcame me. I thought that she was getting preoccupied with the amazing joys of the other side and that I would never have contact with her again.

And then one day, something else changed. I was getting ready to take a walk with my little dog, Cricket, when I heard a bumping sound coming from another room. I followed the sound to the entry hall closet, where I saw that my walking pouch/purse had flown itself out of the closet and was now lying on the floor.

As I picked it up, I said, *Mom is that you? I thought you were too busy!*

And then it happened: I felt her presence and heard her in my mind say, *I'm not too busy.* My heart expanded with joy as I listened to her amazing download of information. I decided to talk with her in my mind as I walked, and it was so touching that tears were streaming down my face.

She explained that she had been in a type of orientation class (for lack of better words to describe it). During this time, everything was explained to her, and then she was given choices. She was reminded of decisions and contracts that she had chosen before this incarnation, and that she had made a promise to incarnate with me and to stay with me. At this juncture, she had a choice, and she told me that she had chosen to stay accessible to me as a type of guide.

Being a mother, she explained, gave her the opportunity to see her children's entire lives. This could also be accomplished by seeing it all at once, because there are no constraints of time and space on the other side. She also explained that she could do everything at once. She could be with each of her children and loved ones at the same time.

Then she said something that touched me deeply: *I'm sorry that I didn't understand your gifts when you were a child, but I understand them now, and I want you to know that because of your sensitivity, I know that you can hear me and communicate with me, and that is why I am staying with you as a guide.*

At that point in my meditative walk, the tears were flowing. It wasn't just the reconnection with Mom or the wonderful news that she would be close; it was much more than that. I could sense this tremendous feeling of joy and peace surrounding her. So many of us long to be of higher consciousness or to be enlightened, and this was it!

There was a fullness of calm warm love around us. She was no longer only the energy of the mother who had raised me, or the brave free spirit who moved to Florida (after her husband's death), or the sweet little lady with dementia, or even the party girl from a few days before. She was something more! She was something indescribable—a ray of light or a bubble of wisdom, peace, and joy.

I knew she was so happy and so settled on the other side. I felt that not only was she not gone, it was as if in some ways she was more accessible to me than she had ever been in my entire life.

As I was walking and crying, the phone in my pocket started going off. It was Ellie, my sweet, sensitive little niece.

Lessons Learned

Empaths have the ability not only to perceive other people's feelings but also to send out strong signals to others. This is one of our superpowers. It can happen when we have strong emotions. Remember, emotions are superpowers, not some kind of weakness. We can send out very strong vibes that other people, especially sensitive people, can feel and pick up. The person often just comes into another's field, and the empath feels compelled to call.

* * *

So my sweet little empath Ellie called, and when she did, she wanted to talk about how she missed Grandma. After a few sentences, she said "Aunt Sandy, are you all right? You sound as if you have been crying."

I quickly explained that it was a happy cry and shared what I could of the recent experience.

She asked me to see if I could get any message for her from Grandma, and I think I did a short reading for her, but like many readings I do for other people, the reading was for her, and it faded away from my memory—similar to the way our dreams fade.

We talked a bit more about how Ellie tried talking to Grandma, and how she wished she knew that Grandma was there with her. Then Ellie asked if there was anything more that Grandma could say to her.

I asked Mom, *Was there something else that you want to tell Ellie, or was your message to her complete?*

There was a pause, and then Mom said, *Tell Ellie to pay attention while she is driving!*

It was *so* like my mom to say something like that, and we both started screaming with laughter! Ellie said, "She's right! I am driving, and I wasn't paying attention because I was crying!" It was one of those magical moments when a beautiful soul from the other side says *exactly* the thing you need to hear in *exactly* the way you need to hear it, to let us know that not only are they still there, but also that they love and deeply understand us.

* * *

One morning a short time later, I was practicing an inner silence technique, which led me to a beautiful meditation. As I entered the inner peace of my meditative workshop (in my mind), Mom was there, waiting for me with my other guides.

She shared with me that even though I was getting information from her, it was coming through me and my mind. So, in a way, I was translating the energy into words. That was why I might download something that I think she would not have said in that way.

She seemed so accessible to me that I asked her all of my questions. I wanted to know why she had to go through the memory loss of dementia the last years of her life.

She explained that this was her soul's way of getting the nurturing that she did not have as a small child. In the nursing home, she was lovingly taken care of. All of her needs were met, and she was bathed and fed and dressed and nurtured.

When she was little, there was only time for survival. Everyone had to pitch in. My grandmother Sadie was an immigrant from Lithuania who could not read or write English. She came over to this country as a seventeen-year-old bride to an older man. His first wife could not produce children after seven years, and in those days, that was cause for divorce.

My grandfather Max wasted no time on that matter with his new bride. Sadie had seven children. He unfortunately succumbed to colon cancer after a lengthy hospital stay. Sadie, my grandmother, found herself widowed at a young age, with the responsibility of six young children to support and raise. So there was no time or ability to give much nurturing.

My mom was only four when her father died, and she already had a baby brother! My grandmother had to run a store, run a farm, cook, maintain a house, make everyone's clothes, and run a bootlegging business just to survive. Mom said that she had so many responsibilities, even as a young girl, that she only had time to do her schoolwork on weekends. After working so hard her whole life, she told me that she enjoyed being taken care of in the nursing home.

Note

Even though Sadie had seven children, one of her sons, Harry, died at an early age of what we believe was leukemia. That is why Sadie had six, not seven children to raise.

* * *

On another topic, Mom explained again that as a mother, she has the gift of following, watching, and staying with her children through their entire lives. Because there is no time and space on the other side, this can be accomplished all at the same time. For my sake, she seems to be available in my time, as I go. She said she could also be with her other children, and others that she chose.

She then talked about our soul group agreement. It seemed that there was a group of women who were nuns in one lifetime together.

They were my mother's mother, my mother's sister, both of Mom's daughters (including me), two of her nieces, one of her granddaughters, and of course, Mom. We made an agreement to come into this life together for mutual support and growth.

Apparently, the exercise of silence triggered a memory of past-life vows of silence and isolation. It explained why many of us have experienced isolation from others and at times from each other. I thought about my own isolation due to chemical sensitivities, one niece's isolation geographically from all of us, and one niece's chosen isolation.

Lessons Learned

Embrace silence and isolation as a gift, and as an opportunity to go inward.

Turn off the TV, music, cell phones, computers, etc. Allow the silence. Ask your questions and then listen.

19

More Conversations from the Other Side

Over the past forty-five years, as I travelled in my meditative journeys and conversed with spirits on the other side, I have come to realize a few common truths. It seems to me that after we die, we often get what we expect—at least initially. We can change our conditions with our thoughts. But some of us are not aware of this fact. We can always manifest what we desire. It is instantaneous on the other side, but the denseness of our bodies slows it down on this side so we cannot see our own creations as clearly.

To illustrate, I will share the story of an extended family member, who I will call Anita. She was a young teenage girl living in Germany during the Nazi invasion. Her mother, who was Jewish, was taken away, and Anita and her father had a horrific time trying unsuccessfully to rescue her. Jewish charities refused to offer assistance because Anita's father was Lutheran. However, Christian charities refused to help because Anita's mother was Jewish.

So, at a very young age, Anita denounced all religious teachings and doctrines. She was probably haunted by those horrific memories her entire life, and she often seemed unhappy. She believed that after death, there was absolutely nothing.

Anita lived well into her upper nineties, and even though we had a nice relationship during her life, it was very quiet after her death. Often, I feel a person's energy and can easily communicate with them, but this was not the case with Anita. I just let her have whatever quiet adjustment period that she was creating, and left it completely alone.

About five months later, I felt that I could tune in and check on her. I reached out by calling her name and saw a visualization that she was stuck, lying in the mud. Her head and arms were visible. She said very clearly to me in her strong German accent, *Leave me alone, I'm dead.*

I was quiet at the realization that someone who was aware and communicating was still very much alive. The silent awakening thoughts were swirling around us. It felt as if we were having a shared understanding without words.

I wanted to show her that she had the power to change her situation. I handed her a single white rose and asked her to just concentrate on that. I then started sending her pictures of beauty in nature, like the energy of trees. I sent her mental pictures of beautiful green grass and flowers and sky. I tried to explain that she could quickly change her environment with her thoughts.

I left her sitting, leaning against a tree, in a beautiful peaceful forest. She was playfully fascinated by a tiny bird that she had cupped in her hands. I felt at peace, believing that she would navigate to a better situation for herself, and let it go.

A few weeks later, I received a large box of family albums. Anita's daughter was cleaning out her own house and thought that we would like the pictures of our side of the family. As I opened the box, one single unattached photo fell out at me. It was a more recent photo of Anita with her two granddaughters.

The thing that struck me was that it was the most vibrant, happy photo of Anita that I had ever seen. It was so beautiful, though I couldn't imagine that her daughter purposely sent it to me. Anita was only extendedly related to us by marriage, and this seemed like a photo that others would want to keep.

I quickly contacted her daughter, who confirmed that it was a mistake, and she didn't know how it got into my box. I agreed to send the picture back, but there was a deep joy in my heart. I got the beautiful thank-you message from Anita that she was happy, vibrant and joyful, with a new understanding of how to maneuver.

Lessons Learned

Remember that we are always creating our own realities with our thoughts. Even though it is slower for those of us who are still in physical form, we are nevertheless creating and manifesting all the time. Practice making good choices.

What are you choosing to do with your precious thoughts?

20

Dreams

When a very close friend was in college, I had a very intense dream about her. I dreamed that she had taken a group of people on a trip. The upsetting part was that it was dangerous, and she had taken these people somewhere illegal.

When I woke up, I was so convinced that something was up with her that I called and asked if she had travelled anywhere that weekend.

"No," she said, and swore she hadn't gone anywhere.

"But I had this dream" I pressed. "You were taking some friends on a trip. It was very intense, and you were taking friends somewhere illegal. It was so clear, and I really felt all these intense emotions."

There was a silent pause, and then she said, "It wasn't that kind of trip. I didn't take my friends anywhere. Though I was with my friends and having an intense emotional experience. The only thing I *took* was mushrooms for the first time."

Lessons Learned

Your dreams are like a secret hidden treasure chest of unbounded information, knowledge, and inner guidance. They can point out things that eluded your consciousness in everyday life, and they can illuminate and help you work out internal struggles. Dreams can be a source of tremendous intuition, and they can help you heal.

If you would like to have more dreams to work with, there are a few prerequisites:

- First, you have to get enough sleep. Even though we have dream cycles all night, it is easiest to access and remember dreams in the early morning after you have completed enough deep sleep patterns.
- Secondly, it is helpful to make your dreams a priority. You do that by asking to remember your dreams and by being committed to writing them down when they appear. Having a notebook at your bedside and recording them as soon as possible is important. The more you pay attention to your dreams, the more they will come. You can even ask for specific guidance concerning a specific issue.

Once you become familiar with your dreams, you will start understanding that you have your own unique symbols. They are yours alone. Spend time in your dream journal on interpretation. If you are unsure what a symbol is trying to tell you, ask yourself, *What does this symbol represent?* Use freestyle writing to write down your symbol and ask, *What is everything that this symbol is to me?* Do the same for people who show up in your dreams.

As you become more familiar with your dreams, you may wish to learn to *lucid dream*, which means to become aware that you are dreaming and start controlling your dreams. It is a wonderful practice for self-enlightenment and healing. In my experience, maneuvering in a lucid dream is similar to maneuvering on the other side. Things happen quickly, as your experience follows your thoughts.

I learned a lot from a book called *A Field Guide to Lucid Dreaming* by Dylan Tuccillo, Jared Zeizel, and Thomas Peisel.

21

Heart Songs

When I was in my early twenties and working as a psychiatric nurse in an inpatient facility, my very first patient was a teenage boy who was anorexic and catatonic. He had gone up to his attic after an assumed bad breakup with a love. After shaving his head, he stared into a candle and would not move, eat, or drink. The only clue was the song "Greensleeves" that was found beside him. He was hospitalized in severe physical deterioration and had to be tube-fed to save his life.

I didn't know that I was an empath back then, however I was leading song groups on the unit with my guitar. I secretly would direct loving energy as I reached out with my voice to merge with all the other voices in the room. It felt as if we were all becoming one as we sang together. I loved that part of my job.

Weeks went by, and this young man was not really improving. With gentle encouragement, I could get him to walk a bit beside me, but he still had to be tube-fed, and he wasn't talking at all. His legs were swelling, and I felt as if I just had to do something to try to get through to him. So, one evening shift, I took my guitar, sat down beside him, and sang the song "Greensleeves" to him.

It's a beautiful song that starts, "Alas my love, you do me wrong, to cast me off discourteously, for I have loved you so long, delighting in your company." I sang with all my heart, directing my love and caring and energy into his heart. I just wanted to reach him.

After I sang to him, I noticed that his nasogastric tube was getting all crusty around his nose. It wasn't my absolute job, but it needed attention, and being his nurse, I decided to take him into the treatment room to clean his face around the tube.

I was lovingly washing his face and nose when he spoke out. His voice was very hoarse from not talking for so long. He said, "Take it out! I will eat!"

I quickly called the doctor, and we had the feeding tube removed. From then on, he ate and recovered, and finally was discharged. I didn't see him for at least a year.

When he appeared in an outpatient clinic where I was then working, I shyly went up to him and asked if he remembered me. I was so startled that I was speechless when he replied, "Remember you! You saved my life!"

The last time I saw him was a long time after that. I was driving in traffic, and I saw him driving past me on a motorcycle, with his long dark hair flying in the wind!

Lessons Learned

As I look back over my life, it's always been about my singing. When I was very little, I imagined that I would be a singer, but secretly, I was afraid that the applause would be embarrassing. Even back then, I knew that my voice was to be for a higher purpose than mere ego. No matter what job I did, I always found myself leading singing groups.

At that time, I didn't know about music therapy, sound healing, or toning, but I did follow my inner calling. What is your inner calling? What do you love to do? What did you used to love to do? What did you think that you would like to do when you were a child, before life got between you and your secret desires and talents?

Follow your heart songs. Do not be concerned if your heart songs sound or look different from others around you. Do not get discouraged if there are millions of others who may have come before you with similar gifts. They are not you, and what you have to offer is uniquely yours.

Your special contribution is needed in the world, and if you do not express it, it will be lost. The world is counting on you to stop hiding behind fear and step up to what you are meant to be doing. The pleasure that you will experience will be worth the risk!

22

Who Am I and What Am I Doing Here?

When I was a little girl, I remember asking my mother questions like, what do you think we are supposed to be doing in our life? and why are we here? She told me that she thought we were here to help each other.

I have asked this question many times in my life. Have you ever wondered about your life purpose? Have you ever contemplated the meaning of your life? I cannot answer these important questions for you; however, I can share the answers that I have for my life. I hope you find them helpful.

Lessons Learned

I believe that we are spiritual beings living in a physical body. Even though it is very hard or impossible for our human brains to process, we are part of universal energy. We come from the same place to which we return. There is no death, just transition from physical to nonphysical.

Everything and everyone is part of the same love energy. (Some call it God or source.) When we decide to incarnate or take on a physical body, it is our choice. We come in with a mission, and it is often for life lessons.

I see it as a great adventure that we agree to embark upon blindfolded, because so much of our memory is wiped away. I believe that my mission is to learn and grow, and to help others.

I believe that it is important to face each obstacle with courage, and to find the joy in our beautiful lives wherever and whenever we can.

Part Two
HANDBOOK

Your Brain's Operation Manual

When you were born, you found yourself in possession of a very complicated, sophisticated bio computer called your brain. However, most of us were never given the instruction manual that explained how to use it effectively. Here are a few basic guidelines when it comes to proper use and maintenance of your brain, and my best advice on how to have a happy life.

23

Concentrate on What You Want

CONCENTRATE ON WHAT YOU WANT, not on what you don't want. Worry is a complete waste of time and effort. Going over and over all the possible things that could go wrong, and then imagining a dreadful future, is counterproductive.

There is power in your thoughts. Whatever you focus on increases in your life, so learn to turn the page or change the channel so that you can dream good thoughts, not nightmares.

Use centering strategies. Also, getting out in nature can really help you change your focus for the better.

Note

Pessimists are rarely disappointed!

24

Get Off the Crazy Train

Going over and over past hurts and tragedies is like getting on the crazy train. It puts you in a victim mentality, and the longer you stay on the crazy train, the more it builds momentum. Suddenly, you have more and more proof of how very wronged you were. You build your case stronger and stronger, and the faster the train goes with the increased momentum that you give it, the harder it is to get off!

The best strategy is to not step onto the train in the first place. When you feel triggered or reactive to what others have done or said, use your breath to return to the present moment. The present is all we have. The past is dead. The future is imaginary.

Do not waste any of your precious present energy on righteous indignation or held grudges. Holding grudges is like being a jailer. For every person you put in prison, you have to carry that heavy key around with you all the time to make sure the prisoner stays in the assigned cell. Those keys get so heavy, and they weigh you down.

Learn to forgive. We are all imperfect souls, here trying to learn our own life lessons. No one is perfect. We all make mistakes. We all see things from different perspectives. Try to walk in others' shoes sometimes and imagine what they must have gone through in their life to be acting as they are. There is your way to do something, and there is my way to do the same thing; there is no *the* way.

25

Listen to Your Words

What are you saying to others, and especially to yourself?

- Are you complaining about something or someone being a pain in the neck, and then wondering why you have a stiff neck?
- Are you experiencing backaches as you think to yourself, "I can't stand this anymore!"
- How about arm, shoulder, or hand problems from constantly saying or thinking, "I can't handle one more thing!"
- Listen to how you talk to yourself. Are you calling yourself names like *stupid, useless, poor, ugly, fat, old, tired, not good enough,* or *lazy*? Wonder about whose voice you might be unconsciously repeating over and over.
- Take control of your thoughts and your speech. Be the master of your thoughts. Do not let your thoughts be the master of you. Treat your body and yourself as you would treat a precious, sensitive child. You *are* precious, and special, and unique. You deserve to be held in the highest regard.

26

Take Care of Your Body

If you want to be happy, you have to take care of yourself. No one else can do that for you, because it is a do-it-yourself job. When it comes to food, eat fresh fruits and vegetables closest to their natural state so that you can benefit from their life force.

Simply put, we need clean food, clean water, clean air, positive thoughts, exercise, gentle sunlight, nature, and good sleeping patterns. Instead of just dragging yourself around and treating your body like a reticent, resistant child, consider spending a few minutes each day checking in with your body. Stop what you are doing, place your hands over your heart, breathe, and ask your body, *How am I feeling? What do I need?* Then pause and listen.

Your body does everything for you. You can spare a few seconds each day to do something to support your body. Nothing else that you think you have to do is more important than taking care of yourself. Your health affects everything else in your life. If you don't take good care of your body, where else will you live?

Note

When you feel as if your body is out of control, start to question and review what exposures you have had recently. Many empaths find that they are overly sensitive to drugs, medications, environmental pollutants, and chemical additives. Getting your body as clear as possible might help you feel so much better.

27

Step Away from the Fire

When overwhelmed, take a step away from the fire. An empath or sensitive person has especially finely tuned senses and can pick up information and signals, as well as vibrations, of which others may be completely unaware.

When you are the most overwhelmed is when you are the least resourceful. That is because you have less access to the problem-solving front part of your brain. Lovingly give yourself a little distance and time to center yourself and process difficult situations. It's OK when unsure to say, "Let me think about that."

Instead of giving yourself a hard time for being unable to cope well in a difficult situation, find a quiet safe spot to relax, breathe, and sort out all of the confusing data. You deserve a loving break!

You also might find that you are overly sensitive to violent media. After hearing, reading, or seeing violent scenes, you may feel haunted as the thoughts replay over and over in your mind. You may even start to feel unwell. If this is the case, avoiding those programs for a bit is another way of giving yourself a break.

28

Be Your Own Guru

I have had the privilege of knowing many amazing teachers, however, the ones who are the most admirable were the ones who taught me to rely on myself, not on them. Please take my advice, and do not give away your power. Put no other person up on a pedestal.

Everyone has strengths and flaws. No one can tell you how to live your life better than your own wise inner guide. Respect and learn from your teachers and elders. Learn from their lessons, but do not follow blindly.

I have learned that even the most acclaimed psychic forecasters are still plagued by at least a 2 percent garbage ratio. That means that most of the time, their intuitions are right on, but occasionally, they are getting garbage. The problem is that there is no way to know when that little bit of garbage is popping up.

This keeps us guessing, for if we knew everything for complete certainty, perhaps we wouldn't live our lives fully. The important thing to remember is that no matter how powerful, famous, or amazing another person may be, always let yourself have the final word. It is *your* life, and no one knows how to live it better than you.

29

Stay in the Present Moment

*N*OW IS ALL WE HAVE. Pay attention to where you are and what you are doing. When you are hungry, eat. Pay attention to enjoying your food. How many unwanted, empty calories are we consuming with unconscious binge-eating in front of the TV?

Do one thing at a time, and concentrate on what you are doing. How many times do we find ourselves lost in a future or past scenario while our bodies are on autopilot? We suddenly wake up as if from a trance and wonder, *Why did I go downstairs? Where are my keys? Did I put that last ingredient in the recipe yet?*

Focus takes practice.

And as for multitasking, you may think you are being productive, but you are apt to make mistakes when you are using your brain energy to keep switching back and forth between tasks. That is why in nurse's training, the first rule we learned about giving out medications was to do one thing at a time, and to pay attention to what you are doing!

30

Go with the Flow

Think of your life as a flowing river. It is easier when you flow with the current. I am not asking you to show a lack of initiative or to take no action. However, life can get very difficult when you try to swim against the current. There are some signs that you may be going the wrong way.

If you start a project, or schedule a trip, or start planning a major life change, and everywhere you turn, there is an obstacle, you may be going against the flow. There may be no convenient reservations and the timing interferes with other commitments, or someone may suddenly fall ill, or there may be a power outage that prevents your next move, or people let you down, or machines break down, or there might even be an accident.

When obstacles pile up, instead of angrily banging your head against closed doors, take a step back and think outside the box. Stop demanding a certain outcome. You might have to let it go for a while. Perhaps there is an easier way to do this, or perhaps it is the wrong timing. When you are in the flow, things come easily. The right reservations just pop up, someone calls with the perfect information, an unexpected check comes in the mail, someone volunteers to babysit the dog, and all the timing just fits. Everything comes to you with ease.

The trick is to pay attention so that you can take advantage of the wonderful way that all of life can flow to you. Some things will more easily come to you if you can release them first. It might not be the right timing. Years after an original wish, you might wake up to see that an old dream has come true.

31

Making Decisions

With all the added input that empaths experience, making decisions may feel overwhelming at times. When you are being bombarded by so much information, you may think that you have to use your rational mind to figure everything out, when actually, the real answer lies in your gut, or your superpowers. If you are trying to decide between several choices, take time to stop and feel into each one. Center, breathe, and then imagine yourself taking one of the choices.

How does it make you feel? Do you feel happy, excited, and joyful, or do you feel queasy and dark, like you are stuck in the muck? Now do the same thing with another choice. Take the path that makes you feel happier and lighter.

A technique suggested by Anita Moorjani, author of *Dying to Be Me*, is to ask yourself if you are making your decision out of love or fear. Sometimes we decide that we have to do something that we don't really want to do because we think it will keep us safe in some way. When I was trying to decide my occupation, I opted to go to nursing school not because it was my passion, but because I knew that it would be a secure way to support myself. I ignored my true passion, which was music and singing, because of my insecurity and fear.

I was never really cut out to be a nurse. It was a tremendous struggle. I went around in a circle in my life that led me back to my passion.

My best advice is to choose love over fear and save yourself a lot of time and aggravation. Also, please remember that when we are stressed, we can lose up to 80 percent of the blood flow in the front, thinking part of our brain. Decisions are best made from a calm, centered place where we have access to our higher senses.

32

Weird Is Cool

I KNOW YOU FEEL DIFFERENT, BUT the truth is that everyone is different. No two people see and experience the world in the same way. We all yearn to just fit in; however, the trick is to embrace your differences, because your uniqueness is what makes you special.

Please remember that your specialness is a gift to this world that only you can give. It is really OK to be you. You are enough, just the way you are.

33

Understanding Ourselves

There are many different kinds of empaths, and having one special gift doesn't mean that you will have others. Shown below is a list of some of the special empathic gifts:

- picking up other people's feelings or physical body sensations
- connecting deeply and communicating with plants, animals or trees
- feeling one's environment or weather deeply, such as knowing when pressure drops or storm fronts are approaching, or predicting weather patterns well ahead of weather forecasters
- telepathy—picking up the thoughts and intentions of others
- communicating with spirits on the other side

Empaths can receive precognitive information in meditations and dreams, or it may just come to them when they are very relaxed, like on a long drive or in the shower. In times of emergency, information may at times feel like a ton of bricks descending. It is often unavoidably clear. Sometimes, this information involves a possible future event.

The gifts that are strongest in an individual often relate to that individual's strongest sensory type. Teachers know that we all see the world and learn in our own way. Some people are very visual. They do better with written instructions. Their eyes are their dominant sense, so they experience the world mainly through their eyes. Other people have an easier time learning through what they hear. They do better with auditory instruction.

A third type of person learns better by sense of touch and movement. These kinesthetic people learn best through doing and feeling. Then there are people who are very cerebral. They process everything in their head.

These sensory types give an indication of a person's strengths. It can be very pertinent information when trying to understand how different empaths perceive the world.

A visual empath may be said to have *clairvoyance*, or "clear seeing." These individuals have an easier time visualizing scenes. They can see things in their head, almost like a movie playing. They are more apt to see colors and other physical manifestations around people and things in their environment. They may receive symbols or written signs in their mind.

A more auditory empath may be said to have *clairaudience*, or "clear hearing." These individuals more easily receive messages that they hear in their mind.

Clairsentience is "clear feeling." These empaths get feelings in their body. They pick up information that comes to them through feeling the strong emotions or physical sensations of others.

The more cerebral types, who are also empaths, may have the gift of *claircognizance*, which means "clear knowing." They have a strong sense of knowing even if they cannot explain it.

One's first empathic experiences often come most easily from one's strongest sensory type, but empaths can learn to develop all of their senses.

Part Three
COMING HOME TO YOURSELF

Practical Techniques You Can Use

If you have ever wondered what it means to be *centered*, it means to be calm, cool and collected. It means that you have learned how to slow your brainwaves to a more productive state. It means that you have full access to the thinking, problem-solving sections of your brain. It means that instead of being in a stressed, reactive, fight-or-flight state, you are in a relaxed, healthy, calm, happy state in your mind, body, and emotions. In scientific terms, it means that your central nervous system is in a parasympathetic healing and digestive state.

It feels good to be relaxed and centered. It is where you want to be before you attempt to solve problems or resolve conflicts with others. It is easier to hear your inner guidance when you are centered. There are many ways to center yourself, and I will be discussing my favorites in this section.

34

Ground Yourself

What is *grounding*? And why is it important?

When I first learned hands-on healing, I visualized the energy coming from above my head and then into my hands for healing, but I only had half the picture! With all of our thinking, many of us have our energy stuck in the top part of our body.

Now I understand that energy needs to move in two directions. Yes, it does flow from above the head, but it doesn't need to just stay in the top part of the body; it must flow all the way to the ground through our feet. And at the same time, the energy needs to flow from deep in the earth, through the bottom of the feet, and then all the way up the body, spilling out the top like a fountain or a whale spout.

Imagine a beautiful fountain of water energy with two main sources. Close your eyes and imagine the energy coming from above your head all the way down to your feet. At the same time, feel the energy from below your feet rising as your feet pull the energy from the earth up your body. Imagine how the energy would flow up the front and down the back. Does the energy spill over your entire body, like a waterfall, where the energies meet?

Many of us live our lives disconnected from our grounding earth energy. We may feel spacey, confused, and wishy-washy because we are blowing in the wind with no grounding.

Did you know that there are approximately one hundred lightning strikes to the earth every second? That is eight million a day! Each bolt can contain up to one billion volts of electricity. There is powerful energy in the earth, and our systems work best if we learn to align ourselves with this earth energy. Our kidney meridian is an energy pathway in our body that begins at the bottom of our feet and is meant to pull the earth energy up our body. Imagine that you are a tree. Feel your roots sink deep into the ground.

Simple visualizations like the examples above, can be very powerful. Below I suggest a few of my other favorite grounding techniques.

The first thing I do every morning is to sit on the side of the bed and give myself a little foot massage. Just by rubbing and stretching the foot, you can start to encourage more grounding. Spend a little time moving and stretching your entire foot. Work around the ankles. Thoroughly rub the bottoms of your feet, and also areas on the top of each foot between the tendons of each toe. Many of your meridians, or energy pathways, begin and end at the end of your toes, so rub each toe.

Spend a few minutes with your feet on the floor. Imagine the energy coming up from the ground through your body and also coming from above and going down to the floor. You can stomp a little or bounce your heels if you want.

Of course, when possible, it really helps to actually be barefoot outside on the ground. However, the mind is a powerful thing. You can ground indoors as well. Even if you are on a higher floor of a building, the building still meets the ground, and then there is a thick foundation that goes deep into the earth. If it helps, you can use the walls of your building to visualize the energy connecting to the ground.

Another little trick that I learned from Eden Energy Medicine is that in order to pull the energy effectively from the earth, we must be in alignment with our polarity. Just as magnets have a north and a south pole, so do we. Using a stainless-steel spoon and rubbing the rounded part on the bottom of our feet for about half of a minute helps our polarity organize itself enough for us to pull the energy effectively.

Definitely try this if you are having any foot issues, or if you feel spacey. It really works. I do this every morning after I rub my feet.

Just as our meridians (or energy pathways) often start or end at the feet, they also start and end at the fingers, so by massaging your hands, you give yourself a little energy boost and help with grounding. Pay attention to your wrists also. By doing both feet and hands, you are hitting powerful points of your energy flows.

Note

If you've ever been to an acupuncturist, you will see how many of the needles they place on the hands and feet. We can access these powerful points ourselves with our amazing electromagnetic hands.

Besides walking barefoot outside, we can lean or sit against a tree. If you really want to have an experience, go to a private place where you can try hugging a tree. Close your eyes while sending loving energy to the tree and visualize the tree helping you ground deep into the earth. Imagine your roots going deep into the earth, where there is a ball of glowing white light energy. Connect your roots to that as you travel back up to the surface. Use that visualization whenever you need to ground.

One of the most powerful and simple ways to connect to the energy below you is to stand with your arms out at your sides. With palms facing toward the earth, breathe in through your nose as you slightly raise your arms while visualizing the energy coming up from the earth with your hands and breath. Try pushing the energy back down with your hands as you breathe out. Keep collecting the earth energy as you do slight flying motions with your arms. You can also experiment with breathing in through your nose and out through your mouth. Envision sending loving, healing energy into the earth.

Grounding is so very important to learn and practice. In my work as an Eden Energy Medicine practitioner, we learned how to check and then balance the energy flows of the body. One of the very first things that we check and then correct is grounding, because when that is off, it affects everything else. Correcting that first can solve a myriad of problems.

Note

Another amazing technique that you can use is to sit on the ground. With your hands touching the earth, imagine that you are plugging in while you send any illness or physical problem deep into the earth to heal. Say a little thank you prayer as if it has already happened.

35

Deep Belly Breathing

Just Breathe

It all starts with your breath. Breathe deeply, filling up your belly as you inhale through your nose. Exhale through your mouth. Inhale as if you are smelling a rose. Exhale as if you are blowing out a candle. I know I have repeated this throughout this book, but that's because it really is important, and it really does make a huge difference.

You can also try taking a deep breath in through your nose and then holding it a few seconds before you blow it out very slowly through your mouth, as though you were blowing through a straw. Experiment with breathing in and out of your nose also. What feels best to you? Making the exhalation longer than the inhalation will help you relax.

As you breathe in, feel your belly blow up like a balloon, and as you exhale, imagine the balloon deflating. Just this alone can relax your nervous system.

You may also enjoy experimenting with other breathing techniques. A lovely thing to do is to count your inhale and exhale during a conscious walk. Notice how the numbers change on their own.

Note

It is easy to get disconnected from our bodies when we are busy with our devices and tasks. Take time to stop and pay attention to your breathing. Our breath reconnects our mind to our body and brings us back home to ourselves.

36

Becoming Present

Feel Your Body

Wherever you are, sink into your body. Feel the weight of it as you lie in bed, or feel the support of the chair where you are sitting, or feel your feet as you take a step.

Be Aware of Your Other Senses

What else does your body feel? What do you hear? What colors do you see? Is there a smell or a taste? Just sitting and listening to the sounds around you is a lovely meditation.

Ask Yourself, Can I Handle This One Moment?

Ask, *Am I safe? Do I have everything that I need right here and now to enjoy my present moment?* Usually the answer is *yes*, unless you are allowing your consciousness to be dominated by demands and expectations based on the dead past or the imagined future.

Be in the present moment, because that is all we really have. If the answer to the question of whether you are safe is *no*, then that is another story. If there is a fire in the house, get out!

Sandy Westerman

Spend Time With Animals and Babies

Very young children and animals live in the present moment. When you sit with them or play with them and really tune in to their world, they can transport you back to your present moment.

> **Note**
>
> Transform moments of boredom by using mindfulness.
> The present moment is a gift.
> That is why we call it the present.

37

Drink Water

We are electromagnetic beings and a very high percentage of our bodies are water. If you want to feel better, keep hydrated. Water helps all of our electrical processes work better.

Every cell of your body depends on those little positive and negative charges working properly. Remember those protons and electrons? Water conducts electricity and connects those circuits. That is why we do not throw a hair dryer into the bathtub!

(Please don't do that.! You could get electrocuted!)

> **Note**
>
> Clean water is a topic for another type of book, but use common sense and avoid contaminated or chemical-laden water sources.

38

Meditation

There are many ways to meditate. Some techniques use a word or mantra that you repeat over and over, while others have you focusing on your breath. I learned to use a creative visualization process from the Silva Method. It is called simply the "Three-Two-One technique," and it is easy to learn.

I describe my revised version below. However, you can find whole courses on the Mind Valley website. Books by José Silva are also readily available. I was lucky enough to learn directly from this brilliant man and his organization.

The Three-Two-One Technique

Level Three

Put yourself in a comfortable safe place where your body can completely relax and let go. Lying down is fine. Close your eyes and imagine that there is a large white screen six feet above and in front of you. Take a deep belly breath in, and as you exhale, visualize the number *3* three times on the imaginary screen.

Also as you exhale, feel your body sinking deeper and deeper. Let your body feel heavy on whatever surface it is lying or sitting. Inhale and repeat. As you exhale, again visualize *3, 3, 3* on your screen as you think and feel deeper, deeper, deeper.

As you feel your body sinking deeper each time, you will start to feel the heaviness of your body and the lightness of the part of you that is counting and watching. Repeat this until you are truly at level three, which is deep body relaxation. Breathe normally after three deep breaths. Other level-three techniques would be to imagine you have an eraser and, starting with your toes, start erasing up your body. (I usually leave my head intact.)

A different technique is to imagine calming violet light washing over you like a shower. Another is to imagine yourself in a lovely tub of relaxing healing light. Again, violet is very calming. In yoga practices, tensing and relaxing muscle groups down the body is used.

The important thing is to use whatever works for you, but continue using the visualization of *3* on your screen. We do this to train your body and mind what level three feels like, and we practice getting there. You can practice anytime once you get proficient. Level three is for deep physical body relaxation, and it is for learning to sink into your body. Once you feel very relaxed, you can try level two.

Level Two

Level two is for relaxing your mind and thoughts. First, close your eyes and get to level three, then take another deep belly breath. As you exhale, visualize the number *2* on your screen three times.

Next, imagine yourself in your favorite safe place in nature. It could be the beach, a lake, the woods, a meadow, a secret garden, or even a hammock in your own backyard. The trick is to imagine it with all of your senses. See the ocean, the color of the sky, the flowers, the trees swaying in the breeze. Feel the touch of the tree bark on your fingers, the cool water on your feet. Hear the ocean crashing, the birds singing. Smell the flowers or the scent coming off the crashing waves. Imagine tasting a wild blackberry you pick off a nearby bush. Get lost in your imaginary adventure.

This is level two. Have fun. You can feel yourself floating in the ocean on an air raft. The important thing is to imagine with all of your senses, relax, and have fun while continuing to see and connect that this is level two, for mental relaxation.

Another very simple technique for reaching level two is to merely listen to the sounds around you. Use your auditory senses to listen to things you hadn't heard before you started concentrating. There is sound in the silence, and you don't need silence in order to meditate. Use whatever music or sounds you find in your environment. Just sitting and listening, only listening, is a beautiful way to relax into level two.

Level One

Once you have achieved level two, you can begin going even deeper to level one. Again, close your eyes and go through levels three and two. Next, visualize your screen and breathe in deeply. As you exhale, visualize the number *1* three times, and feel yourself sinking deeper and deeper into a deeper level of consciousness. On your screen, place the number *10* and start visualizing and counting backward. This time, try inhaling with the number and saying *deeper and deeper* to yourself, as you exhale, with each descending number.

Remember, when you reach the number *1*, you will be at level one, a deeper level of consciousness. This is a wonderful time to say something positive to yourself, like *All is well in my world*, or *Everything works out for the best*. I always have an intention that everything I envision will be for everyone's highest good.

Once you are deeply and deliciously relaxed, place your thumb and first two fingers together. Remind yourself that this is what it feels like to be centered and at level one. The more you practice the Three-Two-One technique, the easier it will be for you to achieve a deep level of calm when you need it. The numbers serve as a trigger for your body to relax.

If you also practice placing your three fingers together, you can teach yourself another shortcut that will help you quickly remember and reenter a calm state. Merely start the process, and your body and mind and emotions will calm down as you visualize the numbers that you trained yourself to respond to. Once you learn to put yourself in this calm alpha state, there are many problem-solving and creative programming and healing activities you can try.

One of the most popular programming phrases to repeat to yourself is, "Every day in every way I am getting better, better, and better." José Silva used to sign his books with *better and better*. If you like this type of creative visualization meditation, look into the Silva Method for more information.

Note

You can easily return to regular consciousness by opening your eyes and moving your body a little. In the Silva Method the instructor always repeated the following as we came out of meditation: *I am going to count from one to five and snap my fingers. At the count of five, you will be wide awake, feeling fine and in perfect health, feeling better than before. One, two, three, coming out slowly now.*

At the count of five you will be wide awake, feeling fine, and in perfect health, feeling better than before. Four, five, (finger-snap) wide awake, feeling fine and in perfect health, feeling better than before.

Part Four

BALANCING YOUR ENERGIES

Calming Yourself in the Storm

Just as we have many biological systems in our body, similarly we have many energetic systems at work. Although the complicated circulatory, respiratory, digestive, muscular, skeletal, endocrine, nervous, lymphatic, reproductive, and urinary systems have specific and important jobs, supporting any one of those systems affects and helps the whole body. It is much the same with our energy.

When we learn how to balance any of our energy systems, it may affect other energy systems as well. Also, balancing your energy will assist with your physical and emotional well-being.

I am going to review a few of the many energy systems that we have in our bodies and the ways they may relate to how you are feeling. When you are feeling "off," first make sure you are hydrated and that you are not having a blood-sugar crash from lack of food. Work on your grounding and then look to your energies.

In this section, I describe ways that you can balance your own energy systems while helping yourself through challenges. Many of the exercises I learned from Eden Energy Medicine.

39

Meridians

MERIDIANS ARE ENERGY PATHWAYS THAT run throughout the body like ribbons or energy highways. They are all connected and, just like highways, are often named after their specific destinations: each meridian is named after the system or organ it supports.

Even though our highways have rest stops that are easily accessible and very close to the main thoroughfare, there are roads that go miles off the highway, deep into the country. Our meridians are similar. Even though part of the energy pathways go deep into the body, there are more accessible areas, called ACU points. These are the same points where acupuncturists apply needles. However, we can learn how to access these areas with our hands.

The meridians are named after the major organs or systems they affect. For instance, learning how to support the lung meridian can help with breathing. However, there is so much more magic than that. Each meridian also has an emotional component. The lung meridian, for example, is often affected by grief. (Have you ever developed a terrible cough or cold after a loss?) By learning to understand and work with meridians, you can feel better physically and emotionally as well. The following is a very important technique for sensitive people to learn.

Zipping Yourself Up

This technique strengthens the energy pathway that runs up the front of your body. It is called the *central meridian*. This helps protect and strengthen your own energies.

Imagine you have a zipper that runs from your pubic bone all the way up your body to your chin, just below your lower lip. Now place both hands on your pubic bone and imagine zipping yourself up tight by moving both hands together slowly up the center of your body. Do it three times, and then imagine twisting your own secret lock on your chin.

Some martial arts students are taught to weaken their opponents by literally looking them down, or consciously trying to unzip them. Of course, I do not recommend that anyone try to do this, because we all seem to get back what we put out. However, the point is that many of us empaths walk around literally unzipped and vulnerable. You want to not only be zipped up but absolutely "unzippable" so no one can unzip you.

The more you practice this, the stronger you will be in securing your own energies. It is especially useful to do it before going into a vulnerable situation.

There is another meridian, called *governing*, that runs up the back of your body, in the same way that the central meridian runs up the front. You can also zip up your back. Start at your tailbone, and with one hand, zip as far up your back as you can reach. Use your other arm and your imagination to connect the zipper. Come over your head and end under your nose. I always zip up my front *and* my back every day.

Tired? Give Yourself a Rub

When you need a little more energy, try rubbing or tapping under your collarbone, in the indent or first intercostal space closest to your breast bone (sternum). *Intercostal* just means the space between your ribs. This important ACU point is an end point for the *kidney meridian*. By working with this area, we help all our meridian energies move in the proper direction.

40

Aura

Your *AURA* is your own protective bubble. It is your energy field or your personal space. Those of us who have boundary issues or problems determining what is ours versus someone else's emotions or pains would benefit from fortifying and strengthening our aura. Here are a few of my favorite aura-strengthening exercises. They are especially helpful to practice if you often feel vulnerable.

Blowing your Bubble

Imagine that you are standing in the center of your private bubble. It is protecting you like a space suit, bringing in what you need, and keeping out everything that does not serve you. Bend your wrists, extend your arms, and push out. Do this in all directions, as if you are stretching and pushing on your private bubble.

Imagine a strong, deep, vibrant color on the outer edge of your aura bubble. What color is your protective color today? Now, try blowing out as you push out and crossing your hands over your heart as you breathe in. Do this several times.

Next, try the same pushing and blowing out, but as you inhale, try to bring energy to your lower abdomen as you breathe in, and cross your hands over this area. See if one area feels better than the other.

These are two areas where some people's auras can get separated a little from the body. This action can reattach the aura, giving you more protection. Imagine bringing your aura snug against your body like a protective blanket. (Remember, even Peter Pan had to have his shadow sewn back on!)

41

Chakras

CHAKRAS ARE SWIRLING ENERGY VORTEXES running up your body. In general, these high-powered energy centers are where memory and emotions are stored. Each chakra has its own specialty.

As an example, our heart chakra is involved in heartbreak and love, whereas our solar plexus chakra is our power center and gets involved in ego issues. Our throat chakra has to do with communication. Did you ever get a lump in your throat when you couldn't talk about something? Or did you ever have a pain in your heart when you felt heartbroken?

Note

The Zip Up exercise in Chapter 39 will strengthen and protect your Chakras. Many of the other exercises in the next chapter will also be helpful.

42

Resolving Common Problems with Energy Techniques

The exercises in this section not only affect your chakras, aura and meridians, but also strengthen and protect your other energy systems. These techniques will help you physically as well as emotionally.

Feeling Disconnected from Your Body?

Hook yourself up.

Place one finger in your belly button and another on your third eye (the place just above where your eyebrows meet). Pull up on both hands gently and try to feel the pulses synchronize beneath your fingertips. If you feel like yawning or taking a big deep breath, it probably worked.

Try holding your top hand with your palm flat against your forehead, with your wrist at the hairline. How does that feel to you? Everyone is different, so it is important to figure out what works best for you with these exercises.

The Hook up Exercise

If you ever feel as if this is not quite working for you, and that you need a little more help hooking up, try squeezing your bottom muscles (or do kegels) while swallowing at the same time. This exercise connects the central and governing meridians, which meet at the back of the throat.

Note

> So many of us get stuck in our head energy and get disconnected from our body. The *hook up* exercise reconnects a powerful energy called the *microcosmic orbit*. It sends swirling energy up the front and back, and around the top and bottom of the body.

Exhaustion

When you are so tired that you are too pooped to pop, your energies may not be crossing over properly. Try grabbing your left shoulder with your right hand. Dig your fingers deeply into the shoulder well, then swipe your right hand across your body to the right (opposite) hip. Do this several times, and then repeat on the other side.

When walking, pay attention to how easily you can swing the opposite hand forward as you walk. Sometimes we get stuck in what Donna Eden calls a "homolateral" pattern. This can happen after an illness that we can't quite recover from. Instead of our energies crossing in an X pattern, they more resemble parallel lines.

When you want to walk but feel too tired, try this little trick:

Go outside and start walking slowly by moving forward the same arm and leg. Walk for six to twelve steps this way, take a breath, and try to switch to opposite leg and arm movements for another twelve steps. Switch back to the same arm and leg pattern for a short while and then see if you can trick your body into walking with the opposite hand and leg. Take a deep breath to move to the healthier pattern.

See which way feels best. You will know it worked when you feel better and more energized, and you are comfortably walking with the opposite hand and foot.

Note

This opposite arm and foot action is called the *cross crawl*. When babies are developing, it is essential that they learn to crawl really well. This gets their energies moving in good habits. Many children with developmental difficulties have to go back to learn to cross crawl.

It is normal to have our energies become "homolateral" when we are sick or ready for sleep. However, some of us find that our energies are in a bad habit of chronic "homolateral", and we feel yucky, tired, and sick on a regular basis. As with any habit, the solution is to keep working at it until your energies get used to a new way to react. Be persistent with the exercises. It really pays off.

Mind Fog

When you find you can't remember things, think straight, easily add in your head, or put words together, you might have scrambled energies. Instead of panicking about impending Alzheimer's disease, try this simple exercise that in Eden Energy Medicine we call the *Wayne Cook posture*. It was named after a man who was helping people who stuttered.

- Sit on the edge of a chair or bed. Place your right ankle on your left leg so that it is resting comfortably on the top of your knee. Grab your right ankle with your left hand. Cross your right hand over and grab the bottom of your right foot.
- Breathe in through your nose as you pull up and feel the tightness in your back as you pull your leg closer to your body. As you blow the exhale out of your mouth, let your back relax and round as your ankle goes back to your knee. Do this four times, then switch legs.

Wayne Cook Exercise beginning

- End by placing all of your fingers together to form a pyramid. Put your thumbs on your third eye (between your eyebrows) and use the same breathing in through your nose, out through your mouth, about three times.

Wayne Cook Exercise ending

Note

I do this exercise every morning. It is especially helpful before a performance or presentation.

Emotional Distress

Hold your forehead with the palm of your hand. When we are in a fight, flight, or freeze response, the blood leaves the thinking, problem-solving part of the brain and moves us into a reactive mode. These are simple techniques to help bring blood back to your thinking brain:

Holding the main neurovascular points

- **For anger**—Hold your forehead and your temples. Using both hands, place your palms on your temples with your fingertips on your forehead.

- **For fear**—Hold one hand on your forehead with the other on the back of your head (behind your eyes).

Hold for Fear

- **For grief**—Hold one hand on your forehead with the other on the top of your head.

Hold for Grief

- **For panic**—Hold one hand on your forehead and the other on the top back of the head (where the head rounds).
- **For worry**—Try covering your face and eyes with your palms on your cheeks and your fingers touching your hairline. (Your little fingers can cross over at the third eye, which is between your eyebrows.) Allow your thumbs to rest comfortably on your temples.

Hold each pose for a few minutes, relaxing and breathing in through your nose and out through your mouth. Experiment with which one feels the best at each moment. You are an electromagnetic being, and your hands can help return the blood flow. When you feel a lovely pulsing, you will know that it worked.

Always pay attention to how you feel when deciding which are the most helpful techniques. Give each head hold a few minutes before switching. The first step is listening to and honoring your own uniqueness.

Stress

This is a concept I first learned from the great author and orator, Wayne Dyer. When we squeeze a lemon, we get lemon juice. When we squeeze an orange, we get orange juice. If we put an apple in a juicer, do we blame the juice machine if the juice is bitter or rotten, or do we think that the juice reflects what was in the apple?

What do we get when we squeeze, or stress, ourselves? We can no more blame someone else for our reactions than the juicer for the type of juice it creates. When stressed, you have a choice. You can blindly react and blame others, or you can consciously respond to any situation.

When we blame our feelings and behaviors on others, we give our power away. When we blame others for our feelings, we are saying that another can control how we feel and react. Keep in mind, that no one has that power over you!

When you automatically react to something hurtful that someone else said or did, usually it is not about that moment at all. Somewhere in your past, there was an incident that is now triggering you in the present. The real trick is to catch yourself when you start to react. This upset that you are feeling belongs to you.

I know you don't want to hear this next part, but the truth is that every upset is a signal that something inside of you is hurting. If you take the opportunity to slow down, breathe, and work it out, it is a personal growth opportunity. Please stop blaming others for how you are feeling. When you feel yourself overreacting in a knee-jerk out-of-control way, try the following technique. It will pop you out of it quickly and leave you back in control, where you can make better choices.

Overreacting, or Just Feeling Terrible

This is my favorite exercise to do when I feel reactive. Take a quiet moment and practice this so it will be something you can pull out and use in emergencies. It also helps with over reactivity to environmental stressors and sensitivities. I learned this exercise from my studies with Eden Energy Medicine. It is called the *reactivity pose*.

Find a quiet spot and take a few deep abdominal breaths in through your nose and out through your mouth. Just this alone will calm your fight-or-flight response. Place your thumb on the nail-bed of your first finger. Just hold it on the side, where it naturally falls. Do this with both hands so that you will be holding up two OK signs.

Getting ready for Reactivity Pose

Keep your OK signs together and place your thumbs on both sides of your temples while resting the remainder of your fingers on your forehead. Relax like this for a few minutes. You can lean your elbows on your knees or a table when sitting, or use pillows to support your elbows when lying down. Experiment with your breath. You might find that switching to nasal breathing is more comforting.

The Reactivity Pose

Note

Why does this work, and what is happening? By touching your thumb and pointer finger together, you are activating two energy pathways or meridians that are connected to helping us release things that we no longer need. The thumb is on the lung meridian, and the pointer finger is on the large intestine meridian. Just as an acupuncturist might access these points, you can give yourself a little boost by holding them.

Your temples are important triple warmer points. This meridian is activated during a fight or flight response, and so by holding these areas, we can calm down the emergency response. The places where your fingers fall on your forehead are called *neurovascular points*. Holding these areas helps bring blood flow back to your front or thinking brain. When we are stressed, we can lose up to 80 percent of the blood flow to the brain. And I think you will agree that we can use all the thinking brain power we can get when trying to solve problems and maneuver in difficult situations.

Freak-Out Frenzy

This is a little routine for getting cool, calm, and collected when you find yourself in a fight, flight, or freeze stress response:

- Start with both hands straight over your head. Imagine that you are holding tight to whatever is troubling you by making tight fists over your head. Blow out hard as you bring your arms straight down the front of your body. (Try letting your breath out with a *shew* sound, as if you are hushing someone strongly.)
- Open your hands, as if you are throwing the problem deep into the ground. Lift your arms to the side and push toward your back as you return to the original position with your hands up over your head. Repeat the fast blow-out two more times. The fourth time, come down more slowly as you complete the blow-out exercise.
- Next, cover your face with your hands. I call this the "Oy Vey" hold. Your palms are on your cheeks, and your little fingers are crossed over the third eye. Let your fingertips rest on your hairline, and let your thumbs rest on your temples. Lightly cover your eyes in order to block out light, but not enough to put any pressure on your eyes.
- Rest like this for a while, breathing in through your nose and out through your mouth. Next, drag your fingers to your temples and rest there for a few breaths. Go over and around your ears, and rest with your chin and cheeks in your hands. Place your pointer fingers behind your ears in that little indent directly behind your earlobe. This point helps balance the vagus nerve while sending calm and balance to your entire body. Rest here

for a little while. Tuck your neck and bring your wrists together if it is comfortable.
- Next, slide your hands down the back of your neck and rest them on your shoulders. Let your fingers reach as far back on your shoulder blades as possible and dig in. Allow your arms to hang down until you can feel the tension release from those tight shoulder muscles.
- Next, slide your hands down to rest at the center of your chest, which is your heart chakra.
- Take a few deep breaths as you sink into yourself. Find one thing in your life that you are so very happy with and grateful for. Concentrate on your gratitude until you smile.
- If there is any stress left, cross your arms with your fingers under opposite armpits. Leave your thumbs out where they normally fall. Rest in this position for a while.
- From there, slide your arms down to give yourself a big hug. Let your right hand rest on the left side of your body, under your breast (your hand will be over your spleen), and place your left hand on your right elbow, with your fingers in the little elbow indent. This is part of your triple warmer or fight, flight, or freeze meridian.

In Eden Energy Medicine, we call this the Triple Warmer Spleen Hug. Any one of these exercises might be enough; however, when you are really anxious, doing them all will really be helpful.

Note

I learned much of the energy-balancing information in this book from my studies with Donna Eden and Eden Energy Medicine. Many have been revised a bit to make them work better for me. That is what you must do also.

If you find that you cannot actually do these exercises, try visualizing and feeling what it would be like to actually do them. Amazingly, it will work for you, and you may feel a deep calm just by imagining. Experiment and learn to communicate with your own energies. This is just the tip of the iceberg. If you resonate with this, I recommend that you look into learning more.

Whereas other energy healing modalities like Reiki use a type of healing hands approach, where the practitioner directs energy to a passive client, Eden Energy teaches practitioners to evaluate each client's individual energetic patterns. We are taught how to assess nine different energy systems and then make corrections. Self-help measures are a large part of the process, because just as we can get into bad habits, so can our energies, and we often need repetition to correct and reverse energy patterns that no longer serve us.

There are wonderful techniques to self-test and to correct your own imbalances. There is a five-minute daily routine that you can learn and then practice every day to keep your energies balanced.

For more information, go to the website *edenenergymedicine.com* or *edenmethod.com*. On YouTube, try looking up "Energy Minute" or "Donna Eden Daily Energy Routine." There are also books, videos, classes, and certified practitioners.

Bonus Exercise

Donna Eden explains that we must create space in our bodies so that our energies can move. Have you ever watched your dog or cat stretch? They seem to instinctually know what to do. This wonderful stretch called Connecting Heaven and Earth will help us balance our energies.

Stand and ground yourself by imagining your feet sinking into the ground. Placing your hands on your thighs and bouncing on your heels a little will help the grounding process.

With a deep inhalation through your nose, circle your arms out and over your head. Exhale through your mouth as you bring your palms together at the center of your chest.

Beginning the Heaven and Earth Exercise

Breathe in through your nose while lifting one arm up and one arm down. Flatten and push with your palms. Add stretch with your head by looking up at your raised hand while holding your breath.

Connecting Heaven and Earth Exercise

Exhale through your mouth as you return palms to the center of your chest.

Switch arms and repeat several times while really experimenting on increasing your stretch.

At the final exhale, end by bending over and allowing your arms to hang down as you fold at the waist. You may bend your knees a little to make the bending stretch gentle as you take a few deep breaths and relax your body.

While hanging over, start tracing sideways eight patterns with your arms.

As you return to standing, trace figure eight patterns up and all around your body.

Be as creative as you like while moving in figure eight patterns.

Note

This exercise can help you in so many ways. Try it when you feel out of kilter or disconnected. It may help if you feel achy or sore in your joints. It helps when you have taken on other people's energies or when you just want to align your own body mind and spirit. Try it when you feel sad or undernourished.

43

Tapping

Learning to tap or use the EFT (emotional freedom technique) is a very good way to center yourself. There are many research papers proving its effectiveness in lowering cortisol and other stress markers. Once you learn, the procedure is quick, easy, and free. I will briefly describe it below.

How to tap out upset or pain:

Always start with the truthful reality of where you are. Tapping is the bridge that takes you from where you are to where you want to be. The first step is to truthfully acknowledge what you are feeling physically and emotionally. Start by tuning into yourself, feeling the problem, and giving the intensity of your upset a number, from 10 for the highest level of pain or anxiety to 0 for no triggering or pain.

Basically, you accept where you are with an opening statement and then start tapping on specific points on your body. These are end points of meridians or energy pathways. There are many end points, but most procedures call for using about eight of them:

1. Side of inner eyebrow
2. Outside edge of the eye on the eye-socket bone
3. Under the eye on cheekbone below pupil

4. Under the nose in the center indent
5. Under the mouth on the center indent of the chin
6. Below the collarbone in the indent, close to the sternum (breastbone)
7. Under the arm where the side bra band falls
8. Top of the head

The starting point is on the side of the hand (the place people use for a karate chop). This is where you say your opening statement three times. It is something like: "Even though I have [this problem], I completely love and accept myself." Or if that does not feel truthful or possible to say, it could be, "I am learning to love and accept myself."

After the initial statement is said three times while you tap with one hand on the opposite karate chop point, you go through the other points, tapping and merely saying how you are feeling. Talk out loud as you tap, as if you were telling your story to a friend. Let the truth of your feelings come out as you tap.

The more emotions expressed, the better this works. You start with the eyebrow point and move through the other points, ending on the top of the head. (It doesn't matter if you do one side only or both sides of your body at the same time.)

After doing a few cycles of verbally expressing your feelings while tapping, shift to *maybe* or *I wonder if* statements to imagine how this could change. Go through a few cycles of tapping until you feel comfortable repeating positive statements to yourself. Give yourself a few rounds of positive affirmations, and then end at the top of your head.

Take a breath and tune in to your original problem. Has your number changed? This is another way to calm the reactive fight-or-flight response and give you back your calm thinking power.

If you feel that tapping might be helpful to you, I recommend that you learn more. It is one of the most effective remedies that we have for PTSD (post-traumatic stress disorder).

To learn more, go to thetappingsolution.com or download their free app, where you can get nice tutorials and choose from a variety of topics to work on. Every February, they put on a free ten-day tapping summit. I have been attending them regularly. In fact, that is how I learned how to tap.

Epilogue

Why is Empath NOT a Four-Letter Word?

When you are picking up strong feelings, information, and physical sensations from all around you, and when you don't know what even belongs to you or to someone else, it can feel extremely overwhelming. Sometimes it might even feel as if you are a ping-pong ball being batted here, there, and everywhere. In the middle of all that confusion, being an empath can feel like a curse, or a severe weakness. When you are scrambled and confused—and others see you as weak, overly sensitive, or emotional and flaky—it is hard to claim your gifts. Sometimes it feels too hard to even think straight.

However, being an empath comes with so very many superpower gifts. The trick is to learn how to center, ground, and connect enough to receive them. You can do it. I know you can—without drugs or other addictions. Believe in yourself, and practice the techniques that I have offered that work best for you.

See from my writing all the times in my life that inner knowing, intuition, and special gifts have saved and protected me and others. Find your special superpowers and nourish them. Listen to your body, and take care of yourself!

I am leaving you with all of my love. As my dear father said to me, "I have complete confidence in you!"

Suggested Reading

Handbook to Higher Consciousness by Ken Keyes

The Silva Mind Control Method by José Silva

Energy Medicine by Donna Eden with David Feinstein PhD

Dying to be Me by Anita Moorjani

A Field Guide to Lucid Dreaming by Dylan Tuccillo, Jared Zeizel, and Thomas Peisel

Being You Changing the World by Dr. Dain Heer

About the Author

Sandy Westerman has a bachelor of science in nursing. As a psychiatric nurse, she led song and dream groups and taught meditation, along with her other responsibilities. Sandy studied the Silva Method of creative visualization to increase psychic abilities under the creator, José Silva. She used her special talents to create a children's theatre program, where she directed, channeled, and wrote original musicals for twenty-five years.

Sandy is a Certified Eden Energy Medicine Clinical Practitioner as well as one of their certified teachers. She has studied the natural world of self-healing for over forty years. As a mother, grandmother, and self-taught medium, her wish is to share her accumulated wisdom and life lessons with other empaths and sensitive people. Sandy lives in Pennsylvania with her husband of forty-five years.

You can visit the author's website at Sandywesterman.com.

Lightning Source UK Ltd.
Milton Keynes UK
UKHW011355150722
405908UK00001B/165

9 798765 227213